SKYSCRAPER

M.A.N.A.G.Ement

Sales Management 101
Training and Teachings to
Build a Solid Foundation
for a Limitless Career

Meghan S. Clarke

BALBOA.PRESS
A DIVISION OF HAY HOUSE

Balboa Press books may be ordered through booksellers or by contacting:

Balboa Press
A Division of Hay House
1663 Liberty Drive
Bloomington, IN 47403
www.balboapress.com
844-682-1282

Because of the dynamic nature of the Internet, any web addresses or links contained in this book may have changed since publication and may no longer be valid. The views expressed in this work are solely those of the author and do not necessarily reflect the views of the publisher, and the publisher hereby disclaims any responsibility for them.

The author of this book does not dispense medical advice or prescribe the use of any technique as a form of treatment for physical, emotional, or medical problems without the advice of a physician, either directly or indirectly. The intent of the author is only to offer information of a general nature to help you in your quest for emotional and spiritual well-being. In the event you use any of the information in this book for yourself, which is your constitutional right, the author and the publisher assume no responsibility for your actions.

Print information available on the last page.

ISBN: 978-1-9822-6102-3 (sc)
ISBN: 978-1-9822-6104-7 (hc)
ISBN: 978-1-9822-6103-0 (e)

Library of Congress Control Number: 2021903920

Balboa Press rev. date: 03/18/2021

To my mom and dad, who made me feel, think, and believe that I could physically or mentally build anything in this life that I desired.

CONTENTS

PART SIX – EMPATHY

INTRODUCTION

In one sentence, I can say with conviction that you would have to be nuts to want a career in management. However, with even more conviction, I will say that it can be one of the most fulfilling experiences of your life.

This book provides foundational training for managers, but it is also a love letter of sorts to a career that has brought me so much meaning. As with any great love, there are ups and downs, twists and turns, and hard choices between right and wrong. Ultimately, where the strong survive, the trained will thrive, and true leaders develop lasting careers.

{ **where the strong survive, the trained will thrive** }

My hope is that when you look back upon your time as a manager that you will have this same experience. Sure, there will be mixed feelings as with any relationship, and some years are better than others. With close to over half of sales managers never getting any management preparation—me being one of them—the statistics are low in regards to not just managers getting trained on the fundamentals, but also how to navigate trying times. How I wish I had a book like this one when I started my career!

In the beginning, I had no idea how many different talents are necessary to be successful. The skills a solid manager needs encompass everything from time management, writing, preparing and making presentations, and doing analysis... not to mention developing interpersonal and people skills to be able to coach a team. Whether in sports or sales, coaching is essential to transformation. Would a football team go into a season without practicing, reviewing strategy, and working closely with the coach to improve? That is where the magic happens. Through consistent feedback via coaching tools reviewed in this book, you will see the performance of your team improve, and also their alignment to you as a supportive manager.

> **management is not about yourself, it is about supporting others**

The work spent coaching your team will lead to subtle changes over time. They may not even realize a transformation is happening until later. The joy will come from watching this growth and knowing you were a conduit to others becoming their best selves. This gift is invisible, but tremendously meaningful. At some point we all realize that management is not about yourself, it is about supporting others.

While support is key, having the fundamental knowledge and tools to coach your team members is paramount. This book, along with the management training academy found at www.skyscraper-management.com, is here to be that support for you.

> **How great would it feel to know you have the tools to be not only a good manager, but a transformational leader?**

As you embark or continue your skyscraper career in management, I want you to feel confident, have clarity through coaching, and build a culture among your team with enthusiastic employees. How great would it feel to know you have the tools to be not only a good manager, but a transformational leader?

Meaning: Meaning in management is hard to define, but absolutely critical. Most successful companies have a mission statement. Why should this be different for managers? It is important to write it out because you will come back to this personal mission statement, especially when times are tough. It is important to know, state, and remember your purpose and passion—why you wanted to get into management in the first place.

Acumen: The first 30 days are critical to starting out on the right foot with your team. It is important to introduce your vision in a way that is not overwhelming or stifling. Whether you are just starting in management or have been in management for years, there are tools and templates to support you as a leader and allow your team members, peers, and executive team to look at you with respect.

Nurture: One of the most trying obstacles in coaching others is that the results are not often immediate. It is the everyday actions taken by team members, combined with accountability from you as a coach, that make all the difference in their growth. Nurturing your team is like

{ Nurturing your team is like planting a garden. }

planting a garden. When the soil is just right, you plant your seeds, water the garden and take care of it, and ultimately beautiful plants emerge. With coaching, you prepare your team's mindset (getting the soil ready), offer coaching and feedback (planting the seeds), do the work by being in the field with them and offering one-on-one calls and coaching reports (watering the garden), and then slowly but surely you will see a transformational change in performance (growth).

Accountability: Accountability and metrics are essential to your team's success. If you do not set expectations up front, your team will never know where they stand. It is also very hard as a manager to hold your team to a standard if they do not have it clearly outlined for them. This section of the book dives into coaching reports, business planning, and other ways you can build that culture for your team. It is not easy to do, but by establishing accountability and sharing your vision, everyone knows the path to success.

G.S.D. – "Getting Stuff Done": Most sales managers spend days in the field and on the road. What you do during that time is crucial not only to productivity, preparation, and purpose. It is also essential to your health, energy, and enthusiasm. Being on the road can be lonely and I will share some tips I learned along the way for remaining healthy—physically and mentally—which is challenging when not at home. Also, tips for what to do with downtime will make all the difference in creating a balanced life at home and work.

Empathy: The most challenging times as a manager can be with employees who have lost loved ones, are going through divorce, or these days, even navigating a pandemic. Helping team members through crisis is nothing you can ever fully prepare for. However, the way you react, respond, and reach out to people during these times makes all the difference. Also, having to terminate employees and verbalize what happened is one of the most difficult parts of being a manager. It literally can break you, so turn to this section of the book when the inevitable happens.

No matter what your tenure, as a manager you will be ahead of the game in regard to coaching reports, business planning, and interpersonal relationships if you can execute the techniques contained here—surpassing other managers and directors with years of experience. Just remember... it is not the number of years that you manage, but rather what you do in those years that makes the biggest difference.

> it is not the number of years that you manage, but rather what you do in those years that makes the biggest difference

My hope is that you will be better prepared for this journey called management. By following the acronym of M.A.N.A.G.E.—*Meaning, Acumen, Nurture, Accountability, G.S.D.,* and *Empathy*—the six sections of this book will give you the foundation to create a skyscraper of a career, one in which you have built a symbolic foundation that will not fall when a storm comes, but that will withstand all the positive and negative experiences that come your way.

A career built on an unfaltering structure will withstand anything, supporting your team as well as yourself. With the right tools and preparation, the height of your skyscraper career is limitless!

PART ONE

M.A.N.A.G.E

Meaning

FLOOR 1

MEANING IN MANAGEMENT

*"Life has no meaning. Each of us has meaning
and we bring it to life. It is a waste to be asking
the question when you are the answer."*

—Joseph Campbell

Meaning in management? Not many people think there is something deeper or even spiritual about management. On the surface, you may believe management is only about directing others to accomplish business objectives. But management can be so much more than that. In addition to the achievement of straightforward business objectives, it also means being a leader, coach, partner, and support system for your team.

Keeping my personal management mission statement in mind has made all the difference for me over the years. Understanding your meaning, your purpose, and your why will become the foundation—the concrete upon which you can reliably build your skyscraper career—that makes everything else possible. Whatever comes your way, good or bad, you will be

Understanding your meaning, your purpose, and your why will become the foundation—the concrete upon which you can reliably build your skyscraper career able to continue to move forward... with purpose, passion, and conviction.

As you will see at the end of this chapter, I will share an example of my mission statement. My foundation. My personal definition of the meaning of management. It may be very different for you. There is no right or wrong personal mission statement. However, when you take the time to discover the meaning of management in your life, you will not just discover the "why," but also unlock the "who."

The why is easier to answer—who wouldn't want to advance their career, have more responsibility, recognition, and in some cases money? But when I say "who," I mean not only who you are as a manager, but as a person. Answering "who are you" and "what is your meaning" will not just translate into your management mission statement, but can profoundly affect who you become as a person.

Self-reflection before jumping right into these chapters will give you confidence and clarity you'll need later. The clarity may seem obvious from your current vantage point, however, when business times get tough, decisions you once viewed as clear cut can later seem distorted and out of focus. Those are the moments when coming back to your mission statement will be critical. Your purpose will propel you.

> **Your purpose leads to passion. Purpose and passion together lead to a career in which you will thrive.**

Defining your personal meaning and mission is like laying the concrete foundation upon which you build your skyscraper career. When that base is built solidly, and you understand your own mission, it will give you the confidence needed to make decisions for not only yourself but your team. When you have a personal mission statement, it becomes ingrained in you. Your purpose leads to passion. Purpose and passion together lead to a career in which you will thrive.

The more you understand your reason for joining management, the easier it will be to make it through any difficult times, and the greater your success during the amazing times. Some days you may ask yourself, "Why am I doing this? I could have made more money staying in sales and only had to worry about myself." When those moments, days, or even weeks happen, remember your foundation, your compass, the reason why you got into management in the first place.

When the hard times have hit me like a tidal wave, I always remember that my goal is to help other people on their journey. I get up every day and go to work for them, to be the positive leader who makes an impact in their life.

So what is your "why"? Here is a little quiz to help you answer this important question:

> *Honestly rank the reasons why you are taking on a management position from 1-5, with 1 being the top reason, down through 5 as the least likely.*

_____ Helping others

_____ Making more money

_____ Title/prestige

_____ Career advancement

_____ Being the captain of a team

There are no right or wrong answers. By looking at your scores, you will see if your management style aligns more with ego or in a desire to help others. If you are taking a management role just for the money or because you feel like it is a natural progression in your career, there is nothing wrong with that. You are just going to have to work harder on the intangible aspects of management—building a culture among your team members. If you are all about helping others, however, you may need to pay more attention to the acumen or business sides of your management role.

No matter what your reasons, it is important to know your foundation and your "why," as these will help identify your personal strengths and allow you to work on your weaknesses.

Whether you are a seasoned or new manager, or even a manager-in-training, you are part of a beautiful yet tumultuous journey that will bring you joy and fulfillment... and sometimes frustration beyond what you believed possible. Kudos for wanting to gain more skills and insight. No matter how many years you have been in management, you will continually be in situations which will teach new lessons.

The road to gaining a management position is often long and rigorous. That goal may have seemed unattainable, and then all of a sudden you landed the job, but now you don't even know where to start. It looked so easy from afar, right?

Most of us have looked at our manager at some point and wondered if he or she was a moron. Of course we could do the job much better! I felt the same way... until that day when I became the inexperienced "moron" who did not know how to put one management foot in front of the other.

This book is gleaned from my own personal experience. It took years to cultivate these coaching tools and even longer to learn how to successfully implement them for the success of my team members. Wouldn't you rather start your career with momentum and confidence?

Management is a race that is won through consistency rather than short bursts

Whether it is Day 1 or Day 1,000, wouldn't you rather lead with a plan in place and the tools in hand to be a success? It is not the manager who is best at sprinting that will be in their position for the long haul, but rather the one who knows it is actually a marathon filled with ups and downs. Management is a race that is won through consistency rather than short bursts, which could lead to burnout, fatigue and quitting.

There is no shame in feeling alone, lost, intimidated, or even scared. In the pages that follow, you will learn best practices for accountability, working in the field or office, using coaching reports, working cross-functionally with other departments, and how to deal with HR (our favorite department... *not!*). You will see examples of coaching templates such as coaching reports, one-on-one call templates and how to have your team execute on business plans. To make it even easier, you will be able to access a few key templates to implement by downloading them to use with your team members at www.skyscraper-management.com. In addition, on this site you can find my management academy, where there is an in-depth training and a library of templates to use to coach your team.

After reading this book you will be able to implement these tools into your coaching and management career to make an immediate impact with your team members.

Disclaimer: Some personnel issues and situations may require humor! You will see and hear things during your time as a manager that you never thought were possible. Through shared examples, I hope it will make you feel more prepared when these situations arise for you... because believe me, they will.

My hope for you is that you will wake up every day looking forward to going to work and supporting your team members' efforts, and taking pride when you see them step on the President's Club stage to win an award or simply make strides in their professional development.

You, as a manager, are a valuable part of your team members' support system, especially during difficult times. If you lay a foundation of trust and transparency, you can change people's careers for the better, holding them accountable and giving them the tools to succeed... even when your team members may not believe in themselves. As a result of this support and belief in your team, your team members will in turn support and believe in you... even when you may not believe in yourself!

As mentioned earlier in this chapter, I think it is important for me to be transparent and share my personal management mission statement before asking you to craft yours. Remember, there are no wrong or right answers here! Take time before you write this. Go to a quiet or peaceful place in your head and heart and take time to breathe deeply. Going deep within yourself is truly what will help guide you when writing your statement.

Here is mine:

My mission as a manager is to wake up every day to support my team members not only to do their day-to-day jobs, but also to inspire them to be the best versions of themselves. I want to be a leader who sets a clear vision, works in collaboration, and encourages others... one who will be strong, a rock, the unwavering foundation... unwavering in both my encouragement of them, but also with accountability, coaching, and drive. Ultimately, being selfless, I give my all to each member of the team when times are tough, and am present to celebrate their achievements and accomplishments in times of success. My goal is to be not just a manager but a leader who builds a culture where team members can thrive and grow. Unrelenting passion for people, a purpose of growth for us all, and a dedication that is constant and consistent will guide me.

What is your personal Manager Mission Statement?

_____

_____

_____

_____

_____

_____

_____

_____

_____

_____

_____

_____

_____

Blueprint for Success:

- Write your personal "Manager Mission Statement" before you move forward to the rest of this book. It is important to know the "who" of the person you are and the "why" for the reasons that you want to either be, currently are, or have just become a manager.

- Think about managers you have had in the past and why they were important to you. How did they make an impact on your life? Also, think about those who were uninspiring or difficult. Reflecting upon a positive and negative manager will help define the type of leader that you want to become.

- Examine your answers from the quiz at the beginning of this chapter and reflect upon them. There are no right or wrong answers, but the simple questionnaire can help to identify areas of strengths and weaknesses.

FLOOR 2

Putting People First

*"The growth and development of people
is the highest calling of leadership."*

—Harvey S. Firestone

As you saw by my personal manager mission statement, my goal each day is to support my team members. This means that I do my very best to put my ego aside and put people first.

Most of the work you do behind the scenes will never be recognized. To put others in front of yourself really means to be selfless. Being selfless necessitates there will be sacrifices to be made, but once a team understands that you have your heart and head in the right place, they will have your back just as much as you have had theirs. That is when the old acronym T.E.A.M. (together everyone achieves more) comes together.

> once a team understands that you have your heart and head in the right place, they will have your back

The 3 C's of Putting People First

The actions of putting people first start with the 3 C's—
Communication, Collaboration & Confidence.

Communication

Any great relationship starts with communication. Each week I have one-on-ones with my team members. I follow a template and take notes on their key activities, but most importantly, I demonstrate that I am listening to them. At the end of the call I always ask, "How can I best support you?"

When you actively offer to support your team members, they understand that you are not just micromanaging with this call, looking over their shoulders, checking what they are up to. Instead, this demonstrates you truly care about what they need to be successful during the week ahead.

Mondays are a great day for this activity because it gives time to answer questions before a situation reaches the boiling point, helps prepare the team for customer calls, and ultimately allows your team to do their jobs to the best of their abilities. Also, you as a leader will be pulled in many directions, so this supportive gesture shows your team members that you are setting them ahead of your busy schedule.

In addition, team conference calls are a great way to connect with your staff as a group, but also where your team members can communicate with one another. Hosting weekly conference calls (I prefer Mondays for these as well) sets the tone for the week.

I always prepare an agenda and send it to the team via email 24 hours in advance so they are mentally prepared for the discussion. Engagement by everyone is key, so I always ask a team member to lead a section of the call. For example, if you have a company newsletter or weekly updates, encourage a team member to read this rather than you speaking for the whole hour. Lately, I have been doing all of my conference calls via Zoom with video. This makes it feel as though we are all in the same room together. That feeling of being together has unified the team.

Collaboration

> Collaboration is absolutely essential so people feel they are being heard and that their voices count.

Collaboration is absolutely essential so people feel they are being heard and that their voices count. There are many instances in which you as a manager can make decisions on your own, but instead, consider asking team members for input. When working on commercial initiatives, marketing materials, and presentations, I usually create an advisory board of 2–3 representatives to get feedback. [Beware however, because having too many people involved can stifle a project.]

This small group knows they are the voice of the sales team, so they often engage and collaborate with their peers. Also, by getting people's opinions and insights on projects, you are getting their buy-in. This is crucial because once you get the team members' support on a project, then it becomes "our" project rather than "Meghan's," therefore, they will be much more enthused and excited to launch this initiative, since they were part of its creation, rather than it all coming from a top-down approach.

Confidence

Making people feel appreciated and supported gives them confidence. When your team has confidence then they will both act and feel like they can do anything. This is why it is so important to take the time to acknowledge all of the positive things that are happening within the team and organization. Sending out positive emails, giving praise on conference calls, and sending cards or personal notes can make all the difference.

There are many things as a leader that you can do to build confidence, but acknowledgment is absolutely key. Recognition for all the positives is meaningful, but also really listen and hear people when any negative situations are happening. When we truly listen and take action in situations that may look like roadblocks, we then become leaders who bring value to our employees. Confidence is not just a one-way street. Your employees need to have confidence in themselves, but it is also crucial that they have confidence in you as their leader.

A Healthy Balance

The way we look at our tasks as managers can often lead to us thinking differently about our positions and ourselves. There needs to be a healthy balance between being firm and managing with accountability and compassion. We will discuss this later in the book, but I have found a way over the years to terminate with compassion by making decisions for employees when they may have not seen that the position was not the best fit for them. This is very difficult and one of the hardest discussions you will make as a manager, but at the end of the day you are in a *leadership* position for a reason, and one of these reasons is to help lead people toward their destiny. Have you ever thought, maybe you are the problem and you are holding this person back by not making the tough decision, taking action and being transparent with them?

Firing or laying off people can be one of the most difficult parts of what we do as well. This will *never* be easy, however, there are ways in which you can do this in a manner that is both humane and respectful to the employee. What's important to remember is that you will never know how the employee will react, so it's going to be critical to have a game plan for how to handle this. We will review keeping to the script, working with HR during these situations, and how to handle the ripple of change and chaos that can ensue within an organization after this occurs. You'll also learn how to best communicate any changes that do occur to the rest of the organization in order to continue to keep people producing, feeling safe, and not falling into the negativity storm that can occur when people feel insecure in their positions and lose faith with their organization.

In addition to tips on management, you will find a chapter on interviewing others and interviewing tips for yourself for management positions (even if you don't have experience). When I became a manager, there was no specific management training, but I worked on projects on my own with my Area Vice President that gave me transferrable experience that I could reference when interviewing for management positions. The attention to detail that I gave to interviewing was key to me landing positions against people with more "experience." I promise, if you follow through with this prep work, your likelihood of winning the position will drastically increase.

Regarding hiring others, I have made a lot of mistakes that you don't necessarily need to make if you follow the steps in this book. Hiring talent can be another of the most challenging parts of the position. I have experience both hiring sales representatives and directors, and what you need to look for in both roles is different, but also very much the same when it comes to core competencies specific to the relative positions.

If there is anything that I have learned in this management journey, it is that people want to be led. This is an exciting opportunity to grow and make an impact in people's lives, but simultaneously it can be lonely if you are perceived as the "bad guy or girl." It is my hope that you will learn through related experiences that there is a way in which to implement "intangible leadership"—meaning how you get other people to perform and do activities without having to mandate, or be forceful, or be a jerk. For some people it is an innate skill, but don't worry—it can also be learned.

$$\left\{ \quad \textbf{people want to be led} \quad \right\}$$

Until your team *feels* and *knows* that you care for them, you will not be able to implement intangible leadership. If you are able to execute on intangible leadership, then you will have team members who will make the extra call at the end of the day, be a part of building a culture of positivity and accountability on your team, and ultimately develop a team that is going to drive revenue and execute. So, let's get started on this management journey together.

Blueprint for Success:

- Communication is key. Schedule one-on-ones every Monday with each of your team members.
- Schedule weekly conference calls and rotate team members taking the lead. Late afternoon Mondays is usually a good time to kick the week off on a positive note.

- Create an advisory board of 2–3 representatives and run projects or initiatives by them to promote collaboration.

- Send out positive emails at least once a week to your team to help build confidence. They will appreciate the recognition.

Visit www.skyscraper-management.com to download a free one-on-one template for your weekly calls. Keep a file for each team member so you can easily review what was done last week, what is coming up this week, and how you can support them.

ONE-ON-ONE CALL

Representative Name:

Date: MTD Revenue:

UPDATE ON ACHIEVEMENTS AND CHALLENGES FROM THE PREVIOUS WEEK

1
2
3

KEY STRATEGIC GOALS FOR THIS WEEK

1
2
3

KEY APPOINTMENTS FOR THIS WEEK

1
2
3

CHALLENGES AND OBSTACLES YOU ARE FACING

1
2
3

HOW CAN I SUPPORT YOU?

SKYSCRAPER
M.A.N.A.G.Ement *Academy*   SKYSCRAPER-MANAGEMENT.COM

PART TWO

M.A.N.A.G.E

Acumen

FLOOR 3

Your First 30 Days

"The only impossible journey
is the one you never begin."

—Tony Robbins

I can still remember the day I learned I was going to be promoted from a sales representative to a district manager. It was everything that I had wanted. After multiple President's Club wins and accolades, it seemed like the natural progression. I mistakenly believed it would be "easy" to coach others to get the results that I had. The thought of leading a team absolutely captivated me and I was ready to make the leap from sales to management... or so I thought.

Looking back, I really had no clue what it took to be a manager, let alone a successful leader. How naïve I was to think it was going to be an easy road and that I finally "made it." Do we ever really make it? The one thing I do know is that I had no idea what I was getting into when I received that promotion. Not only did I get my first role in management, but oh yeah... I needed to move to Houston from Miami in two weeks without ever visiting Houston in my life. Taking on my first management position would be challenging enough, but to do so in a new state where I knew no one really shook me to my core.

I can still remember that fateful day when my life was about to change. It was a beautiful, sunny Friday in Miami, and I was winding down my day driving to Mt. Sinai for one last sales call before heading into the weekend. As I was cruising over the I-395 bridge, staring at the beautiful turquoise water, I received a call from my Regional Vice President who was the catalyst for getting me into management and to whom I will always be grateful. I had an inkling I was going to get one of the three management positions that just came open—San Antonio, New Orleans, or Houston. He was excited to share the news that he was promoting me to Houston.

As I looked at the shimmering water around me, my heart sank. I have had a long love affair with Miami, one I still can't fully shake. The minute I'd stepped off the plane from California at age 17 for a college volleyball recruiting trip, I was in love. The thought of leaving the city that was now home to me broke my heart. All I could think was… *Isn't this what I always wanted?* I mean, I had finally made it… right?

At that point I was 31 years old and it was just me and my Labrador, Grady. Without a spouse at that time or children, the decision was all up to me. So, over the next couple of weeks I packed up my things, said goodbye to customers and friends, and cried my way up the turnpike. I felt alone, scared, and just wanted to turn the car around and head back to my little townhouse in Coconut Grove and pretend it was all just a bad dream.

As I moved along the I-10, it took me until Louisiana to come to the realization that this was indeed happening and there was no turning back. Thank goodness I didn't turn around! An amazing adventure was awaiting me in Texas, a state which I have grown to enjoy and respect.

Luckily, before I left Miami, I met with my mentor who had years of management experience. It was great to land the position, but what would I do the first day, week, month, year?! Thank goodness I asked for help, because my mentor made it very clear what I needed to do in order to start off my new position on the right foot. The advice that he gave me is still pertinent today and I use it whenever I start a new position.

Tip #1: Use a prepopulated template

This territory business overview template should be focused around key accounts, customers, and areas of the representative's business that you should get to know as soon as possible. This exercise is really two-fold. It is critical for you to prioritize the most important business needs of your region while also understanding the representatives' business—the top accounts, key people within those accounts, any obstacles, and ways you can support your team members immediately. Not only will you be able to learn about the key accounts more quickly, but it will show the representatives at the very start of your partnership together that you care about understanding their business and want to learn how to best support them.

This activity will go a long way to starting off on the right foot with your team, showing them that you took the time to understand their needs, and want to contribute to helping them grow their business. This is the first activity you can do to build trust and credibility.

There is nothing worse than when a manager, or anyone in a leadership position, arrives and has the attitude that they "know your business" already. I can tell you from experience that no two jobs in sales or in management are the same. When you start as a new manager, be open, humble, and willing to learn. In the first 30 days it is critical that you get in the field or find time in the office with your reps and observe and ask questions. Then take that information and correlate it to your own experience and start coaching from there.

In a previous position, I worked with a VP in marketing who talked about what he did 20 years ago selling a product that was not even remotely similar to our product portfolio. Not only did it make him seem like an old timer, but he lost respect and legitimacy since he did not care to get out in the field and learn about our business. He brought *no value!* Do you want to be known as a leader who sits behind a desk pontificating on the good old days? Your team members want to know what you are going to do to make a difference *now*. People can smell BS a mile away, and just because you have a title does not mean you are respected. You will need to earn that respect and confidence. When

> just because you have a title does not mean you are respected. You will need to earn that respect and confidence

you follow these easy steps, you will set yourself apart from all the other ego-driven mediocre managers out there. You will stand out and make a difference!

Tip #2: Have a team conference call

Set up a conference call with your team the first week of your new position. You are going to be nervous and your mind will want to talk you into waiting… but trust me and do it right away! Your team knows your start date and is waiting to hear from their new manager. This is crucial. But don't worry. You do not need to have all the answers. In fact, being transparent and saying that you are new to this position and want to learn will go a long way. This will be the team's first glimpse at your leadership style. Setting the tone quickly will show your team members that you are excited to be their new leader and work with them.

In every company, team members question, "How did this manager get hired?" I have heard it all, and sometimes the chatter is offensive—for example, for me it has been filling a female quota—this does happen but don't get upset. Instead, stay true to yourself and your game plan. You only have one chance to make a good first impression. Check your co-dependency at the door or you will be constantly questioning and beating yourself up. Stay strong and true to yourself!

> Check your co-dependency at the door or you will be constantly questioning and beating yourself up.

On the first conference call, your team members are going to be just as nervous as you are. A million questions will be running through their heads such as "Is this person going to micromanage me?" "Does this person understand our business?" and "Is this manager a jerk / intelligent / understand balance and the importance of family life?" They are already imagining a worst-case scenario that you will make their lives hell. During this first conference call, simply talk about your background and ask each person to introduce themselves, then ask how long they have been with the company, and to share a couple interesting facts about themselves (meaning spouses, kids, pets). The most in-depth you want to go is to give them a timeline of the first month and what you want to accomplish, including:

1. Working in the field or in the office with your team members at least 1–2 days and reviewing their territory business overview template. This is where you bring up the template you are going to send for them to fill out that will have an outline to follow where they can fill in pertinent information such as their key accounts, customers, obstacles, and opportunities. The goal is to gain insight and clarity on their business and start formulating ideas on how you can be a resource for them.

2. Observing their business firsthand and understanding it more in-depth before setting team expectations and rolling out your coaching tools. Usually, I recommend doing this after one month at the very least in the position. Seek to understand their business first before setting expectations that may or may not be inappropriate for this business.

During my first management position, I made the mistake of coming in guns blazing on that first conference call and rolled out team expectations and what each person was going to be responsible for—weekly routing by 8:00 AM, quarterly business plans, time off requested in the payroll system at least a week in advance, work hours 8AM-5PM each day, etc. All these expectations were acceptable, but do not do it on the first call! It will immediately turn off your team members and you'll become unpopular like I did.

A more preferable and positive way to do this is after you discuss your main objectives during the first 30 days in the position, such as working in the field with team members and reviewing their business plan template, then you eventually roll out team expectations. This will put your team at ease and you will not come across as a crazy micromanager. After that first month you will gain trust and momentum by spending time with them and taking the initiative to understand their business better. Your team members will appreciate your efforts and it will be the start of a productive and transparent working relationship.

When I did that first conference call, I was managing people who were older than me and some even had previous management experience. After I rolled out expectations without taking time to get to know my team members' businesses first, one individual—who is now a good friend—lost his temper and raised his voice on the call, challenging me in front of the group. I would have driven back to Miami that night if I could. Thoughts of quitting ran through my head. With time and patience it is possible to salvage any missteps. But your start as a manager will be much stronger if you are upbeat, positive, show interest in your team members, and simply set the tone of what is going to occur that first month in a casual yet professional way.

Tip #3: Learn who has responsibility in each department

It does not matter if you came from a different business background than your representatives. Find a way to show them value at the start of your time as their manager. If you can identify specific people in corporate that you can reach out to for answers to your team members' questions, you will look like a hero in a short period of time. Show them that you can and will make their life easier by taking the extra workload off their plates by simply getting questions answered for them.

This is something I have always made a priority when starting a new position. Within the first 1–2 weeks, plan a visit to corporate headquarters if possible, or at the very least set up conference calls with the head of each key department. Sit with key sales support departments such as customer service, operations, marketing, finance, human resources, and accounts payable. Ask questions, be engaged, build rapport, and show that you will also be an asset to the folks at corporate as well. The old line "help me, help you" is a perfect phrase to summarize what needs to occur when you meet with your new cross-functional counterparts. These relationships are key to the day-to-day activities that are needed to support your team members.

If it sounds like you are in public relations or running for a public position and need votes, well you are pretty much correct. You are never done proving yourself and showing value to both your internal and external customers. (Just for clarification, *internal* customers are those departments and team members at corporate who are equally as important as the *external* customers in the accounts where business is being done.) First impressions with your internal customers at corporate are also crucial and will be critical to not only your success but that of your team.

> **both you and your team will accomplish so much more because you put effort into building corporate alliances**

Just as there are reps and managers you will like more than others, your corporate counterparts will also have preferred sales managers. Demonstrate to them that you have a good attitude and are solution-oriented. Like any relationship in life, be kind, humble, giving, and respectful. This will go a long way and both you and your team will accomplish so much more because you put effort into building corporate alliances.

I would like to conclude this chapter by saying that you should always ask to speak to your direct manager within the first 1–2 days on the job and ask them what their expectations are for you during the first 30-60-90 days. You want to make sure that they feel like they have the control, and simultaneously you are then telling your boss what your plans are in these first 30 days by reviewing the points above. In particular, that your goals are to understand your team members' businesses by giving them a template to fill out with key information about the territory, scheduling time to meet and learn more about the key initiatives of each department, and scheduling time to work with each of them. If you go over these action items and share what you want to accomplish, your boss is going to be very impressed that you have such a detailed and well thought out plan.

To be honest, your plan will probably be way more in-depth and strategic in terms of what needs to be accomplished than what your boss has prepared (or not prepared) for you if you follow what we discussed in this chapter. Just don't tell your boss that.

Blueprint for Success:

- Hold a conference call the first week in your new position. Create an agenda to follow and send it 24 hours in advance to your team members. You will be nervous, and this will help the flow of the calls.

- Set the tone by letting them know you are going to work 1-2 days with each of them, whether in the office or in the field. Remind them the goal is to learn, understand their business better, and review their territory business overview template that you are sending to them to fill out before you meet so you can understand how to best support them.

- Send out the territory business overview template that highlights "key territory information" to each team member who will need to fill it out within your first week on the job. Preferably you want to have this activity completed in the first 30 days of starting your position.

- Schedule time with key departments and personnel at corporate headquarters or via conference call. There is no better way to immediately start supporting your team members and bringing them value than by connecting with the "go to" people that you will need to work in collaboration with in order to be successful in your position.

- Schedule time with your direct hiring manager and set an agenda for the call. Ask about their expectations for your first 30-60-90 days. Prepare your own thoughts, especially for the first 30 days, as you want to leave no doubt that you are hitting the ground running. You will not know all the intricacies of the position yet, but this is a great exercise in order to facilitate collaboration and get key insights from your boss.

FLOOR 4

Walk the Walk & Talk the Talk

*"Each person holds so much power within themselves
that needs to be let out. Sometimes they need a little nudge,
a little direction, a little support, a little coaching,
and the greatest things can happen."*

—Pete Carroll

In my opinion, there is nothing more important than coaching and time spent in the field or in the office with your team members. This is your most critical role and responsibility. Not only do you need to spend time with each team member, but you need to bring them value and "coach them to excellence"—building not only a productive team who meets and exceeds quotas, but one filled with individuals whose careers you help transform.

My own career is an example of such positive transformation, and it happened because of the time and effort my managers spent coaching me. In fact, if it were not for being put on a Performance Improvement Plan (PIP) years ago when I was new in sales, I would not be where I

> In fact, if it were not for being put on a Performance Improvement Plan (PIP) years ago when I was new in sales, I would not be where I am today.

am today. I share this story with transparency so you know that it is nothing to be embarrassed about. If a team member's numbers and performance are not where they need to be, there is hope. Time after time, I have seen the extra effort from both manager and representative pay huge dividends. Not only can negative behaviors change, but in many cases such assistance leads to a President's Club win or significant growth in numbers the following year.

> **To coach well takes effort and most managers do not put in that effort.**

The turnaround in my career was thanks to a manager who was often described as a "micromanager." Now, as I look back, I realize she was very intense because she cared. To coach well takes effort and most managers do not put in that effort.

It might be for reasons of not wanting to invest that much energy, or more likely it's because the manager has no idea what "great" coaching looks like.

When I made a change from the pharmaceutical industry to medical device sales, my past achievements left me feeling overconfident. But in a new sector in the medical industry, I quickly felt overwhelmed and lacked the ability to sell. There were multiple specialties and care settings and, quite frankly, I was so stifled I really did not know how to even open up the conversation with a simple probing question, let alone bring out a marketing piece, go through features and benefits, and close a sale.

After just a few months, I thought the manager was a moron, the company sucked, the training hadn't properly prepared me for my role, and on and on with the excuses. I remember the moment like yesterday—I was put on a performance plan. Now, that may seem a little quick, but to play devil's advocate, if you know someone on your team who is struggling, then it is much better to act quickly.

It was a defining moment in which I decided that I was going to accept coaching. Instead of mentally checking out and beginning a new job search, I dove in headfirst and followed the advice from my manager. Not only was I quickly taken off the plan, but I ended up winning President's Club the following year. The activities that I worked on with my manager were well thought out and reflective of the areas in which I needed to improve.

For example, practicing using simple open-ended probing questions, knowing the top marketing pieces and how to utilize them during sales calls, having a field sales trainer who could mentor me and work with me in the field, and my manager pushing me on sales calls to step outside my comfort zone made all the difference in my performance. I soon learned that if I put the work in and did these exercises my manager asked of me on a consistent basis, then my sales performance and trajectory of my career would change.

Walk the Walk

Have you ever had a manager who spent more time behind a desk "acting" busy than getting out in the field and working with you? Likely you never developed respect for that manager. If you are going to talk the talk, then you also need to walk the walk with your reps.

> If you are going to talk the talk, then you also need to walk the walk with your reps.

Set the tone for your team by being in the field or in the office and working hard together.

This sounds simple, but most managers do not do this. I have always set the tone by working at a pace in which my team knew there was no one working harder than me. It became clear we were in it "together." You can create a culture on your team where mediocrity and laziness are not to be accepted, without even having to say anything. Lead from the front and bring your team along with you on the ride. You can't expect that your team members will be out there hustling if you're only dictating from behind a desk.

Whether in the office or in the field, with today's technology, most emails and calls can be replied to between appointments during the day when you are working with a representative. There is nothing worse than a manager who is on the phone all day emailing, texting or on conference calls, and not engaged with their employees and customers when they have planned appointments and time to work with their manager. From a representative's point of view, not only is such a manager being extremely rude, but that person is also wasting the rep's valuable time.

When you go to the time and effort of working with your team members, be present. This means, when you are in the passenger seat of the car riding with them or sitting with them in the office observing calls, be engaged in that moment. This time is rare, as many managers only get to have the allotted two-day coaching sessions with their team members once per quarter. Those days can be exhausting, but they will go a long way in building a relationship with that team member. As managers in leadership positions, we owe it to our team members to give them our all when we are with them. Most of the time, these coaching visits are only two days and in some instances only four times a year. There is no reason that engagement can't be present or at the forefront of these visits.

I have heard stories about managers sitting in the lobby of a hospital while a representative was in the Operating Room, texting while being on sales calls, emailing and not looking up from their phone while they were in the passenger seat of that representative's car. Quite frankly, it came across as discourteous and disrespectful.

Bearing that in mind, know that it is much easier to navigate a territory or an account without someone else tagging along. If you accompany your team in the field or make time to work with them in the office, make sure you are engaged and bringing them value. One bad ride-along will gain you a reputation not only with that representative, but also with the rest of the team, sharing that you are a hindrance rather than a help.

Coaching Days / In-the-Field Days

So, what does a "good" field ride or coaching visit look like? The answer is that you want to spend *two full days* in the field, or in the office if you have an inside team, at least once a quarter with each team member. Almost any sales representative can pull it together for one day and look like an all-star. Reps whose numbers are down and who know they are not cutting it will still have the ability to pull off a great one-day ride along, taking you to visit customers they probably see or talk to all the time. Even reps who are underperformers have customers who like them and will sing their praises. These will be their go-to customers during your time together. If you are paying attention, you'll notice the same customers who are usually doing very little for the rep's sales will keep coming up repeatedly in conversation. The rep will schedule visits to only these customers since they have not developed their territory.

Instead, you want to schedule a two-day ride-along, from 8:00 AM–5:00 PM, jam packed with multiple calls that are already set up beforehand, to visit sites where you are being brought along to make an impact and be utilized as their manager during the call. Typical days in the life of your representative are what you want to observe. Not a day that they pull together once a quarter which is not a reflection of how they are truly working. If you are asking yourself whether 8 AM is a little early to start working together when accounts are usually not open, remember it is a great time to meet and have a cup of coffee and talk about the key objectives for the day, review any key reports, or answer any questions from the representative. It sets the tone that these two days are important and that you as the manager are there to be a support to this team member.

How do you ensure that the ride-along is going to be packed with these types of impactful appointments? You do this by asking for an agenda ahead of time. An agenda should be filled with the day's activities and appointments, a background of the specific customers, the purpose behind why the call is being made that day,

> **Set expectations that the representative needs to send the agenda to you 24–48 hours in advance of your ride-along.**

and any other pertinent information that would be useful for you to know before the call takes place. Set expectations that the representative needs to send the agenda to you 24–48 hours in advance of your ride-along.

The agenda is just as much for you as it is for the rep. You want to know the times, what accounts and customers you are meeting, and the meeting objective(s) so you can be as prepared as the representative, or more.

Tip #1: Demonstrate the agenda's value

Show your team members that the agenda is not just busy-work. Use information provided within it to do your own research beforehand on the accounts and customers you'll be meeting with. For example, in medical sales, I made sure to research the physicians, the practice, their procedures, schools they attended, hospital affiliations, and any clinical research they had done.

This will go a long way toward the success of the call and also demonstrate a valuable skill of relationship building. You will quickly become a manager your reps will want to work with and bring along on calls. Remember, *you* always need to be showing value, not just the representative. A customer perks up when they get asked questions about themselves, creating a great start to any call. Your representative will also be appreciative that you took the time to do more than just fill out a "report card" on their performance in the field, but rather to help them build relationships that can lead to increased future sales.

> **Remember, *you* always need to be showing value, not just the representative.**

When you don't get the agenda beforehand

When you request an agenda from your representatives, I highly suggest sending a sample of what a "thorough" agenda looks like so they have an idea of your expectations, and understand how you will be using the item before and during your visit. Personally, I use a pre-filled agenda that is an "example of what good looks like." I review this on a conference call within the first 30-60 days in the position so they can see clearly what the expectations are for a well done agenda. After you review this document and send it to them, then there should be no excuse for this not being done. That said, if it looks like the coaching visit is not well planned and is going to be a waste of time, use the days as a coaching lesson on future expectations.

> **By demonstrating the importance of preparation, you encourage greater success, both during and after your coaching visit together.**

The agenda should be reflective of the structure you build for your team. By demonstrating the importance of preparation, you encourage greater success, both during and after your coaching visit together. These habits that you are getting your team accustomed to should aid them to use these tools consistently in their positions, not just when you have a coaching visit scheduled.

There is nothing that bothers me more than a day where my time has been wasted, when I am driven all around the rep's territory on the longest route possible in order to kill time. If the rep doesn't have appointments set up for face time with customers while you are there, then what are they doing when you are not there? I can tell you what they are doing… they are making 2–3 calls a day that are not impactful, wasting the company's resources. But ultimately, their numbers are your numbers, and your numbers are your boss's numbers. Never forget that your team members' performance is not just a reflection on themselves.

Show the rep an actual example of your expectations. If your team member has not given you an agenda or it's lackluster, even after you have coached them with samples and explained the reasons behind its usefulness, then you need to document this. In your coaching report there is a space to note the behavior under "Territory Management." In addition, an email should be sent to the employee stating that they are not meeting expectations. Also, if you later do any merit or performance appraisals, you can refer to the email or coaching report with specific details about what occurred, and check to see if progress has been made after the issue is addressed.

No "free" lunch

When a rep picks you up in the morning and immediately asks where you want to eat that day, this is a red flag. These are typically not the people you want on your team. What's wrong with lunch? No one loves a meal more than me, but the most successful reps and managers are more worried about selling than sitting down for lunch during the middle of the day. Consider alerting your representative beforehand that lunch will be somewhere quick like a Panera. Do not give in to a decadent multi-course lunch that wastes valuable time. Your team members will mirror your actions and behaviors when you are not with them.

The old phrase "There is no such thing as a free lunch" is true in more ways than one. If you set the tone, and that tone is to hustle and make the most out of your day, then your team members will in turn become more productive, have more sales, and be able to buy lunch wherever they want when they're on vacation... because their commissions are so good. Neither of you will be making money dining at Morton's... unless of course you're having a business meal with a customer!

Tip #2: More to Prep than Just Power Bars and Trail Mix

At this point you have done your prep work researching the customers you are meeting with. But how else are you prepared? It is important to you for your reps to be prepared with marketing materials and pertinent literature, then you need to be prepared yourself.

> if it is important to you for your reps to be prepared with marketing materials and pertinent literature, then you need to be prepared yourself

Before the sales call even starts, your rep should be able to go to their trunk and pull out their materials from a portable file cabinet that is well organized with categorized materials. Better yet, the materials should already be prepared in a marketing binder. If I as the manager am more prepared than the rep (which has happened many times) then either they get it and it never happens again or there is a problem and it gets addressed in the coaching report. An inside sales representative should be familiar with marketing materials and I ask they create a binder as well. Usually, they will send follow-up emails with the marketing materials, but it is helpful for them to learn the content of these materials just like an outside sales team member would.

Even if you work for a company where you have the time to coach after the fact (meaning speaking about what piece "should have" been brought out and used), to me that merely prolongs the sales cycle. Instead, coach by example, showing your reps firsthand how to use the marketing and literature pieces appropriately during the sales call. Not only does this help make calls more impactful, but it also shows your team members that there are no excuses for not taking the extra time before the day starts to make sure they are prepared.

Tip #3: Create a Marketing Binder

Create a binder with clear sheets where you can store and easily share marketing materials. This will look professional, plus most binders come with a notepad and area for additional storage of items. Before I venture out on a coaching visit with a team member, I always make sure to re-stock the binder with materials so I am prepared during our time together. I recommend you coach your sales members to do this, and if you also manage managers, then they should have their own binders and know the materials just as well as their team members. After all, how can you coach someone else on how to use the materials if you do not know them yourself?

Before you start with the process of making sales calls together, talk with your rep about the possibilities of sharing duties if a moment comes up during the meeting which might lead to an opportunity to sell. Show respect to your team member and verify that you are indeed there to help and support them, but also offer to step in during the call if they get stuck. Your goal is not to overtake the call, but if there is an opening to demonstrate how to effectively use certain material to better connect with the client, then take the time to help forge that stronger connection.

Use the opportunity as a teaching moment. There is nothing better than real world examples and coaching "live." If you have coachable representatives, then they should be able to implement the exhibited behavior on their future calls and during the next ride-along.

Blueprint for Success:

- Spend at least 2–3 days from 8:00 AM–5:00 PM in the field with your representatives at least once per quarter. If you are in an office, keep these same hours. It is possible to coach and be equally as impactful in an office versus in the field.

- Request an agenda to be returned to you 24–48 hours before a field visit. If you do not receive this agenda, then use the experience as a coaching opportunity the first time you are working with the representative in the field. If the second field ride comes around and they do not provide you an agenda, then cancel the ride-along and document this in your employee's file and via email. Set the tone that both you and your representative's time is valuable.

- Make sure to send a pre-filled agenda template of what "good" looks like before you start coaching visits with your team members. Hopefully, you can review this within your first 30 days in the position so they understand your expectations.

- Be prepared with marketing materials in a binder for your coaching visits together. You should be just as prepared (or more) than your representatives for your field visits together.

- If you are going to be in scheduled meetings with key customers, do your homework and research on these customers in advance. This adds value to the sales calls, and your representatives will be impressed you took the time to prepare. Also the customer will appreciate that you value their time and made an effort to get to know more about them.

FLOOR 5

Essential Skills

"You have plenty of courage, I am sure.
All you need is confidence in yourself.
There is no living thing that is not afraid when it faces danger. The
true courage is in facing danger when you are afraid,
and that kind of courage you have in plenty."

—The Wizard of Oz

Imagine that it is time to make a presentation in front of the executive team, board members, or even your own team and you are not fully confident in your delivery. As a manager you will often have to speak in public in front of key members of the organization, and while doing so, remember numbers and pertinent information in order to be impactful.

Imagine spending hours or days putting together the content, rehearsing, crunching numbers. You thought you were fully prepared for this important event, but now you realize your PowerPoint is a poor reflection of all the work you have done. No one understood your key points because they were squinting at tiny print, lost amidst poor formatting, and you hadn't thought to add any visuals to support your messaging.

What went wrong here? You prepared, you knew the content, and you even managed not to be nervous to speak in front of others. The answer is in your Microsoft acumen and computer skills—acumen that will be critical to your success as a credible manager.

How much better would it be to feel confident that your visual presentation will reflect all your preparation? Don't let a lack of basic computer and presentation skills hold you back from excelling in your management career.

> **Don't let a lack of basic computer and presentation skills hold you back from excelling in your management career.**

MS PowerPoint

Countless times, as I prepared my management team for meetings, I needed to ask for their presentations beforehand. Their PowerPoint skills were non-existent. These were managers who came with years of experience from big companies. Trust me, having to spell-check and re-format presentations before a big meeting is *not* what you want to do with your time, but making sure the presentation will be a success is always a best practice.

Looking incompetent in front of senior management comes at a huge cost. It is immediately detrimental and causes you to lose credibility when a wonky looking PowerPoint pops on the screen. If your fonts are too small and the sizes are inconsistent, if slides are filled with too many words or have numerous spelling errors, no matter how well you know your content, the visual will disrupt your audience and leave a negative impression.

Tip #1: Take a course or read a book about how to create and present a successful PowerPoint

What I most often see with PowerPoints are issues with formatting and overloading the presentation with too much verbiage vs. inserting appealing visuals and charts that carry impact to convey a message faster than words. There are a plethora of ways to get pointers and tips to make a PowerPoint appealing. YouTube, Coursera (online courses) and books can give you the 101 on how to make your presentations the best possible representation of the information you are conveying.

Tip #2: Buy a slide advancer with a laser pointer

Always keep it on you as you never know when you will need to present. I have been in board meetings where no one had an advancer, and in such a case you save the day and look abundantly well prepared. The last thing you want to do is get up in front of others and awkwardly click through slides via your computer manually. You want to be able to walk around and move freely while clicking through the slides seamlessly.

Tip #3: Work with someone in your marketing department who creates impactful PowerPoints

Ask them the tips and tricks to make visually appealing presentations. Make sure you are always using your company-approved templates with color-scheme and company logo.

Tip #4: Snipping tool

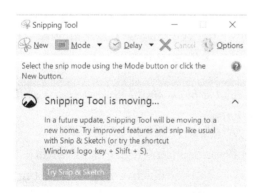

The icon for this useful application is a pair of scissors called "Snipping Tool." Long gone is the messy copy/pasting of information once you master this easy tool. Now, rather than making pivot tables and using import/export, the data can be "snipped" beautifully into a presentation using the snipping tool. That little button will be transformative in your creation and execution of amazing presentations.

MS Excel

MS Excel and all its magical formulas is also a necessary tool for you as a manager to understand and use on a consistent basis. My years in management have been with both large and small companies. While in large companies, reports are often sent by sales operations and there is not such a need to be an expert at Excel, but when working in smaller companies this skill has been critical for me to be able to run the analytical part of the business. It is not an exaggeration that your ability to make strategic decisions around hard data can be the difference between profit and loss. Also, looking competent vs. incompetent with your analytical skills.

Tip #5: A picture is worth 1,000 words

If you really want to impress people, while simultaneously making your data more meaningful, employ simple bar charts, pie charts, Gantt charts, and so forth. Everyone from your representatives to your peers will notice your acumen as many managers do not take the time to learn these skills. By no means is this a "have to," but in today's competitive environment it will be nothing but positive.

Tip #6: Take at least a basic Excel class

Coursera is a great resource that is inexpensive and has a range of topics on courses that will help ground your skyscraper career in management. There you can learn most of the key reports you will likely run using Excel.

For example, on a weekly basis you should be sending and reviewing reports that are pertinent around the metrics that your team needs to hit in order to meet individual and team objectives. In sales, the most common reports would be a top accounts list, revenue report, units in use, and a pipeline of quotes. This will help you keep your team on the path toward their goals and help focus and target where they are spending their time.

Tip #7: Send out key reports weekly

You and your team members need to understand how their actions are (or are not) meeting the performance objectives of your team. Share these reports on a weekly basis. Seeing their performance documented in vivid color and numbers will usually spark them to make better targeting decisions and stay focused on top accounts.

Tip #8: Teach your team how to run their own reports

Make sure to put a filter feature on the reports so they can easily filter through the data in Excel. When you first start managing your team, have a call where you show your team members how to run these reports themselves, so they do not get dependent on you. I usually like to send reports out early Monday morning so I can review with my team on our Monday one-on-one calls.

MS Word

It may seem basic that MS Word is a program everyone would know, especially in management. However, this is not the case. Most documents are still emailed in Word.

Knowing simple sentence structure is important as well as the formatting of paragraphs.

Tip #9: Thou shalt use Spellcheck

Using the Spellcheck feature should be *mandatory* on documents before you send them out. For an additional thirty seconds, visit the Review tab and click "Editor" for a series of simple recommendations to clean up a document tremendously. Whether it is an agenda, resume, or memo, it cannot be stressed enough the importance of using Spellcheck. (This is also important for email and PowerPoint.)

BONUS: Create your own Word document templates, framing the document and adding company colors, to spruce up your documents and make them look even more professional under the "Design" tab in Word.

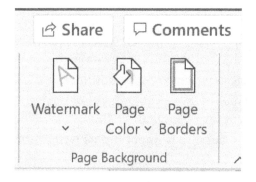

PDFs

Tip #10: Save to PDF rather than .doc

If there is information team members or customers should not be allowed to change, simply save your document as a PDF. This will give the document a cleaner look and ensure that whoever you are sending it to cannot make changes.

Email

Lastly, the same concepts regarding Spellcheck and acumen come into play with emails.

Tip #11: Emails should be short and sweet

If an email comes in looking like Tolstoy's *War and Peace,* I typically do not read all of it. If you have multiple points to be made, simply list them in bullets.

Tip #12: Make sure the tone matches your message

Words can be interpreted many ways, coming across in negative fashion when that might not have been your intent. Choose your words carefully when crafting emails, especially when conveying your message to a large group of people, or communicating with someone new. Remember that some people are more sensitive than others!

Tip #13: Don't put anything in writing that you wouldn't want to see on the front page of the newspaper

Emails can be dangerous and detrimental as they "live" forever. If there is something sensitive that you need to communicate, pick up the phone and talk to that person. My thought process around company email is to write emails as if the CEO were reading them.

In all honesty, you never know who can or cannot read your emails. If there is anything you would not want your boss to read, then use the phone. Share this tip with your representatives as well.

No one knows this better than myself, as I have printed many emails I received that were inappropriate and kept them in a folder for a "rainy day" (if you know what I mean). Protect yourself by both not sending out any emails you will regret and by printing out emails that you receive that may be inappropriate. Unfortunately, you never know when you will need them.

Tip #14: Never hit "send" when you are angry or frustrated

Wait 24 hours if you have a questionable email that is created with emotion. Often, you will find after those 24 hours that the email should not be sent. This is one of the biggest lessons I have learned in my career.

Blueprint for Success:

- MS PowerPoint, Word, and Excel are the three most pertinent programs to learn in order to be successful in management.
- If your skills need to be improved, there are plenty of ways to learn more about these programs. YouTube, Coursera, and books all have information which can help to improve your skills.
- Use bullet points in emails and documents to highlight important points.
- Tone is important when sending emails. If you are writing an email and feel negative emotion, wait 24–48 hours before sending.
- Never put anything in writing that you would not want your CEO to read on the front page of a newspaper.

PART THREE

3

M.A.N.A.G.E

Nurture

FLOOR 6

THE PASSENGER SEAT

*"When you encourage others, you boost their self-esteem, enhance
their self-confidence, make them work harder,
lift their spirits and make them successful in their endeavors.
Encouragement goes straight to the heart
and is always available. Be an encourager."*

—Ray Bennett

One of the greatest honors and privileges in my professional career has been spending time in the passenger seat of various team members during ride-alongs or coaching in the office. Now the passenger seat can be literal, but also figurative, as it really means spending the time with your team members and creating an environment for nurturing growth during your two-day coaching sessions. It does not matter if you have flown cross-country to ride with someone or set aside time to hear their sales calls in an office; both can be equally beneficial.

As managers we plant seeds that need work to be cultivated, but in the right environment growth will occur. When a seed is planted, a flower does not just grow overnight. The seed has to have the right conditions to thrive. Without the proper environment, it grows only a small bit… or not at all. But the goal is for that flower—the team members you manage—to both grow and flourish.

Sustainable and permanent growth requires coaching, dialogue, and consistent attention. Getting to know more about your team members and their lives is truly an honor. If you are an empathetic and transparent manager, you will be able to relate to what your team members are going through and be a rock for them during times of hardship. You will know about their children, pets, spouses, hobbies, births, deaths, and any other major occasion that happens in their lives. This is when your bigger purpose—something beyond just the job description—comes into play.

> **If you are an empathetic and transparent manager, you will be able to relate to what your team members are going through and be a rock for them during times of hardship.**

The way that you support your team members will also be the way that they support you. Do not ever take that for granted, thinking that you do not need their support or compassion, because there will come a time when you do. And it will be the most valuable gift you could ever receive.

Remember the management mindset: We get up every day and work for our team. When you buckle the seatbelt, be aware that whatever is going on in your team member's life will usually show up in one way or another during your time together. Be interested, engaged, don't get too personal. Encompass a healthy balance of humanness, professionalism, and most importantly empathy.

> **The way that you support your team members will also be the way that they support you.**

When you are in the passenger seat of the car, this is when a major amount of coaching takes place and is also a time for you to be able to jot down observations from the call you were just on. Take note of relevant information plus anything new going on in the territory or follow-up items. But don't spend your time on your cellphone catching up on emails. Engage and take advantage of the invaluable face-to-face interaction. Make the most out of your time together. Those emails can wait! Ride-alongs and time spent coaching employees usually happens only four times a year and you owe it to your team and yourself to give it your all.

Tip #1: Carry a notepad and pen

Bring your marketing binder with notepad so you can jot down notes to remember what was discussed during your time together. Maintain accurate details and notes. These details will eventually end up in the coaching report. (We will get more in depth on coaching reports later in Chapter 8.)

Print the pre-set agenda your team member should have sent to you 24–48 hours before meeting, and have that with you to jot down notes beside specific account/customer information for easier documentation in your coaching report. I usually use both so I can have a detailed and impactful report for my team members. Also, it makes it easier to re-cap the visit afterward and document which customers were spoken to, what the call objectives were, and if those objectives were or were not met.

Most of the time your field visits and coaching time will be pleasant with standard calls, taking notes, providing feedback and coaching... but then there are some visits where the person next to you can turn crazy. Oh, yes! In the past, people have started yelling at me, using the steering wheel with their knees, speeding and skidding through snow and ice, staring at the GPS on their phone when they have been to the accounts "hundreds of times," exhibiting road rage and threatening to take out their gun on someone... need I go on?

As I get older, I wish I would have learned about setting boundaries earlier in my career. If you ever feel uncomfortable—or your life is in danger—depending on the severity, ask to be taken back to your car, or dropped off somewhere safe. Then take notes including dates, times, and locations on your cellphone to document the activity. Documenting is one of the worst parts of the job, but it is something I have learned the hard way that is necessary and part of being a diligent manager.

Perhaps the biggest mistake is to think that if you are close to someone you manage, they would never do anything against you. But when employees are being put on a performance plan, laid off, or fired, you will see a side of them that you never thought existed. This will not be every employee that you go through this with, but you will always remember the handful of employees who exemplified this behavior.

Tip #2: Save any negative feedback until the end of the day

When you are working with team members and have to discuss something you know will be upsetting or will not be taken well, do this at the end of the day—preferably when you are either parked or at a coffee shop and can speak to them when they are paying attention. Always keep safety top of mind. Remember, you are the manager and are the one who is supposed to make sound and rational decisions for both parties.

Much of coaching is about delivery, so make sure, whether it is good or bad news, that you are in an environment in which the employee can fully grasp, comprehend, and process the information.

Coaching during a ride-along is an important component to the success of your time together. There are templates you can access for pre- and post-call questions to ask your team member for reflection. They should be familiar with these templates and should be introduced to them via a team training or conference call.

The representatives should make it a habit to use these tools not only when you are with them, but also when they are on their own in the field. Promote self-coaching on your team and coaching themselves after the call takes place. Continual growth will occur for the representative when you are not with them if they do this.

Your reps will likely find the pre- and post-call review process annoying and not want to do this exercise, but management is not a popularity contest. The best reps I have managed usually welcome this extra step in their daily routine, especially those who want to improve quickly. Be sure to treat these reviews as not just check-the-box activities, but well thought-out tools to help in their success.

Tip #3: Be consistent

Use the pre- and post-call templates consistently during each ride-along. If you do not show the value in them, then your team members will not see the value in them. If you are not consistently using them on every call, then

> You are responsible for building buy-in from your team.

your team will not be consistent in using them on their own. You are responsible for building buy-in from your team.

Positive reinforcement should be encouraged. When a success story occurs from using these tools, then have the rep share with the team via email or on your team conference call. Ask them to cite specific points on the exact steps they took using the tools, then share the positive outcome. This will get more immediate buy-in, as no one wants to feel left out on something that will help grow their business.

> When a success story occurs from using these tools, then have the rep share with the team via email or on your team conference call.

Peer pressure does not stop when we are no longer teenagers. Use this positive reinforcement as a way to leverage support for activities you ask your team members to do. This goes for all the coaching tools, including pre- and post-call templates, routing, territory plans, pipeline management, and inputting notes into a CRM. Your team members will at first see this as extra work and possibly even micromanaging. The key is leveraging support from those who use the tools and find success. Visibly recognizing their success, and having them share the way they used the tools, will drive utilization and adoption among the other team members.

Tip #4: Take accurate and detailed notes

Use a standardized template for pre- and post-call notes and agendas. During your time together in the field, fill these out completely and keep them handy when it is time to do your coaching reports. Any documentation from your time together will be helpful when you are trying to remember specifics of what occurred during the visit.

Representatives want specific feedback from your time together and they want it in a timely manner. There is nothing more frustrating than having your manager give you feedback if it is not accurate.

Even worse is when it is delivered weeks late. This can cause team members to view you as dishonest and you will lose credibility.

A good rule of thumb is to deliver coaching reports or feedback within seven days. If you are traveling home on a plane or staying in a hotel after the field visit, use that time to write up coaching reports while it is fresh. Then follow up on any action items from the visit together with a sense of urgency. The longer you take to give feedback and coach your team members, the longer you are stalling their growth.

Your representatives will appreciate that you took the effort to do this in a timely manner, and if there are any follow-up coaching items you want your team members working on, then the sooner the better. Put the effort in and be proactive in providing accurate and impactful feedback to your team members! If done correctly, you will see positive changes.

Blueprint for Success:

- Always carry a notepad and pen or other mechanism to take notes during coaching visits. This way you can write down specific notes and action items during your time together.

- Reinforce coaching tools and templates such as the agenda for the ride-along, returned to you by the representative 24–48 hours before the visit, and pre- and post-call note taking together during your time together. This will make for a very productive and impactful coaching visit.

- Always put safety first. If you have to give negative feedback or unpleasant news, wait until the end of the day when no one is driving. It is not fair to either of you to risk safety.

- People are capable of doing crazy things—always remember to document, document, and document!

FLOOR 7

OBSERVING THE SALES CALL

"A coach is someone who tells you what you don't want to hear,
who has to see what you don't want to see,
so you can be who you have always known you can be."

—Tom Landry

It is obvious by the topics in this book that coaching—and coaching well—is important. This is where the magic happens, transformation occurs, and where revenues are gained. If you coach well, it will turn into a positive team culture, higher commissions for both you and your team members, and ultimately results. This is why you were hired, and that is to meet and exceed expectations not only of your team, but also of the corporation you work for. It all starts with coaching, and one of the first steps to understanding where you can help your team members comes through observation.

> **One of your jobs as a manager is to be a liaison between the customers and corporate headquarters.**

When observing sales calls, whether in the office, via Zoom or the phone, or out in the field in accounts, it is important to bring value... value not only to the representatives, but to customers as well. One of your jobs as a manager is to be a liaison between the customers and corporate headquarters. This means following up on action items for the customer within 24–48 hours. Not only will the customers be thankful, but your representatives will also appreciate the effort and welcome you spending time with them and their customers again.

This often means sometimes having to be the "bad guy." For example, whenever there has been an issue with customer service, tough negotiations, or any problems that have occurred in an account, I always tell the representative that I will be the person to apologize and take accountability for any issues from corporate. This then frees the representative up to not have to take the fall for corporate issues when they are the face of the company to the customer. This proves to be very helpful and appreciated.

Before the call even begins, it is important to remember that the representative is going to be nervous having you with them. You want to do everything possible to alleviate their nerves and show that you are a team working together. Ways in which you can show this are by helping to set up any equipment if you are doing a presentation together, helping to carry in lunch or breakfast for an office, or putting out marketing or other materials before an in-service presentation. This shows that you are indeed a supportive manager and an equal member of the team.

Also, what you wear during a field visit is important. Confirm the dress code with your representative before the day of the visit. Should you wear scrubs for a medical visit if you are in medical sales, a suit for a key appointment, or is the dress code business casual? Especially if your territory spans a region of the United States, it is not likely you can go home and change. It is important that you fit in wherever you are going. There is nothing wrong with asking your team member what is appropriate to wear in their territory. In this way you will not stick out as the manager or "businessperson." Rather, you will blend in and feel part of the meeting.

In addition, keep in mind that different geographies have different cultural norms. In the Northeast, people speak quicker, while speech is generally slower in the South. When I moved from Miami to Houston that was a huge lesson to me on the importance of understanding your environment. In a small town outside of Houston, I walked into an office and there were animal heads and cowboy pictures all over the office. At another point on calls in the South I was asked, "So are you the Yankee?" I had no idea what was meant by all of this, but learned a lot about how others view "outsiders." Remember, you are always a guest in others' accounts and territories. Overall, I have had nothing but positive experiences in the South and in different regions of the United States. I learned that it was more about me being cognizant of my biases rather than any by the customers.

> **Remember, you are always a guest in others' accounts and territories.**

When in an account, it is important to remember that every customer is equal and should be treated respectfully. You never know who the decision maker might truly be. Often the front desk person can make or break access to an account. Be upbeat and friendly, saying hello, but also making sure to stay out of the way and not be disruptive. The office manager or whoever is running the account is sometimes a spouse. Be conscientious that this person may makes decisions in the account even though it is not necessarily the doctor or someone in a "C-suite." The last reflection you want to be is as someone who is awkward or unfriendly.

Another part of observing the sales call is what you are going to do to make sure that you are not sitting there documenting every word that was spoken, but just enough so you are able to keep the feedback factual. I had a manager once who lurked in the corner with a notepad in hand during the entire sales call, capturing every word both the customer and I were saying. This made the customer feel very uneasy. It will also make your reps feel on edge… which creates a non-productive sales call. Remember, your team members should *want* you to ride with them and work with them in the field! If you sit there like a court stenographer, it is a surefire way to make yourself very unpopular. As an engaged manager, you should be able to remember key points that occurred and write them down in your pad when you get out of the call.

Keeping proper documentation can happen when you get to the car. Let your team member know before the ride-along starts that you will be taking notes and doing a coaching report, ensuring them that you care about their development and that your time together is productive and beneficial to their sales future. Overwhelmingly, your team members will appreciate you took the time to give them constructive feedback.

Tip #1: Include one or two quotes in your notes

To show you are listening deeply to the conversation and not just paraphrasing, include a quote or two in your field notes. You do not want to record the whole conversation though. For example:

> When the customer said, "I am currently buying my disposable products from Company B," you replied, "OK, thank you for that information."

Then you can get into what could have been done differently, such as:

> *When you replied, "OK," you could have said, "What*
> *is it you like about Company B that makes you buy*
> *their products from them?"*

This is a very simple example of how you want to model your coaching both during and after the call, as well as when writing a coaching report. Write what was said verbatim in quotes, and use supporting verbiage to the conversation. Then this will become part of an opportunity to coach these actual observables.

Tip #2: Stay engaged during your field ride

If you are a field manager, put aside thoughts about your later flight, the amount of emails that are piling up, and where you are going to dinner that evening. If you give your team members everything you have—both mentally and physically—your time together will be more impactful and lead to greater growth for that team member. Also, your team member will feel valued and respected.

What NOT to do

Have you ever had a manager who was a complete embarrassment on your sales calls? One who cut off your customers, interjected at the wrong times, verbalized inaccurate product knowledge, was on their phone… Well, you obviously don't want to be one of those managers!

When you are with your team members it is important to mirror their behavior and bring value. Now that I manage managers, I have had countless representatives tell me their managers do not bring value on sales calls and sometimes they are an embarrassment. Inevitably, no matter how seasoned of a manager you are, mistakes will occur at one point or another. But foresight is always helpful.

Here are some tips of things NOT to do:

- Do not arrive late to work in the field with a rep and then leave early.

- Do not review emails or texts on the phone while in the presence of customers/clients.

- Do not neglect to know the product information and make up answers that are inaccurate.

- Do not interject in a conversation just to speak instead of remaining silent if there is nothing pertinent to say.

- Do not be condescending to customers or others within the account.

Bottom line, know your surroundings, bring value to the call, and for goodness sakes, do your research on the customer. If you are going to speak, then seek to understand the customer first so you can then begin the process of understanding how best to help.

Blueprint for Success:

- Bring value during sales calls by being engaged in each moment of the interaction.

- Follow up on any requests or action items from customers within 24–48 hours of the visit.

- Ask your representative about the dress code before the ride-along.

- Take notes once you are in the car, with a couple of quotes to help support your observations and feedback. This will help your representatives to accept and take action on any areas for improvement.

- Take note of both positive and negative observations; it should be a healthy balance of both.

PART FOUR

M.A.N.A.G.E

Accountability

FLOOR 8

THE POWER OF COACHING

*"People can't live up to the expectations
they don't know have been set for them."*

—Rory Vanden

Coaching reports document the competencies and observable behaviors of your representatives in the field or in the office. This is the report you complete as a manager after a coaching visit, documenting the actions that took place, as well as any coaching and follow-up items that need to happen next. This activity is one of the most important things you can do to positively influence the actions and behaviors of your team members.

In earlier chapters, we discussed the agenda you should require your representatives to send you 24–48 hours in advance. We also covered the importance of taking notes so you can properly document a coaching report with accurate observations. Also, that two full days either working in the office (if your sales team is on the inside) or in the field (if your team is made up of outside representatives) is optimal. Many companies, especially larger and more structured ones, will have standardized documents for you to fill out, but for uniformity in this chapter, we will work with a coaching template that I created and used for years that reflects the most important competencies to measure and observe during your time together, also the most critical traits for the future success of your representative.

This template can easily be tweaked for any sales industry, but there are four main sections that are universal: *Territory management, Competency, Sales skills,* and *Feedback/follow-up.*

When adjusting this template, first fill in whatever section titles pertain to your business. For example, Clinical Competency could be interchanged with Business Acumen, Industry Knowledge, or simply Job Competency. These four sections will build a robust report, reviewing all the most important aspects of the position with the ability to document observables in each section.

The final segment—Coaching Recommendations & Follow-up— is tremendously important. If your representative is struggling with opening the conversation or understanding the pain points of a customer, for example, you could provide feedback such as:

> *"Please develop 5 probing questions by August 5 that are open-ended and will help start the conversation. We will review these during our one-on-one call on August 12."*

To me, this is the most important section of the report, as this is where the magic happens to truly transform the performance of your representatives!

Now let's dive in-depth into each of the four sections of the actual report.

Blueprint for Success:

- Have a standard coaching template that you use with each representative for consistency. Review this template on a team conference call before you start your coaching visits so your team members know what competencies you are looking for and why they are important.

- Update the core section headers with verbiage that pertains to your specific industry.

- Before the coaching visit begins, ask the representative what parts of the sales process they feel they most need to work on to prioritize your time together. Often this will line up with your observations, but it will make your team member more inclined to take action since it was their idea.

SECTION 1: TERRITORY MANAGEMENT

Territory management can have many different names, but how a sales representative runs their geography, territory, time, customer base, and leads should really all be the same. What you are looking for is how they are managing their business.

Key observables to note in this section of the coaching report include:

- time management skills
- routing
- the agenda for the ride-along
- business planning skills
- targeting
- expense report submission in a timely manner
- resource/expense management
- report/data utilization
- pipeline management

Nothing is more important than where your representatives are spending their time and how they make use of their days. For example, in medical sales, you will likely have sales reps who will take you to an account where the front desk staff tells you: *"The doctor is on vacation (or in surgery) right now."* This will be one of your greatest frustrations as a manager. If the rep nonchalantly blows it off when they get back in the car, then you have a problem.

> **Nothing is more important than where your representatives are spending their time and how they make use of their days.**

You want to document this immediately and let the representative know they should have called the previous week (or at least the day before) to assure the customer would be in the office before driving an hour to make a call. It takes only one minute to do this versus an hour wasted on an unproductive visit.

If your representative does not have an agenda prepared for you 24–48 hours before the ride-along, or it is not well thought out, this is the section where you would document it in the report.

If they do indeed have a well thought out agenda with set calls and appointments, then make a note here as well. Positive feedback is just as important. If reps are doing the key preparation that lends itself to a positive ride-along and productive time together, you want to recognize them for making both your jobs easier.

If you have a position like mine, where you are away from your family and spending most of your time on the road, then you should do everything possible to ensure that time in the field is productive. If your reps can't put together two productive days with you, what are they doing when you are not there? You know the answer!

These days, many companies have Customer Resource Management (CRM) tools such as Saleforce.com or NetSuite. If your representatives are responsible for logging notes after calls or creating leads in the CRM, then this is where you would document whether or not they are meeting expectations. In order for feedback to be useful, your team members must be aware of their target goals each week, so you can hold them accountable.

> If your reps can't put together two productive days with you, what are they doing when you are not there?

For example, if they need to log 20 calls per week with notes, then this area of the report is where you would add commentary. Most representatives do not like this part of the job and look at it as "big brother is watching." However, companies spend a large amount of money on CRMs and it is our job as managers to keep reps accountable for meeting expectations.

Salesforce and other CRMs make it much easier for representatives to generate reports to assist their targeting efforts. For example, representatives should run reports weekly, or look at those generated by their companies, on their numbers and account data. Based on these facts and figures, it is easy to justify where—or where not—they should be spending their time.

If your team members are not using data and just going out in the field or calling customers aimlessly, then they are wasting time and company resources. Top account data, top accounts, revenue, contract data, and affiliations should be looked at daily or at the very least weekly. Adjust to whatever is pertinent to your industry, but make sure your team members are viewing reports and looking at data to make wise business decisions.

Tip #1: Fix the basics

When most representatives first get started in a territory, they tend to forget the basics. Coach them to call on the top 20% of accounts first, gather business cards for each customer, note the times and days of the week when the customer is in the office, and use the CRM tool (if your company has one) to back up this data.

Starting to document what days and times are best to see their top accounts and customers is the #1 activity your representative can begin with to make sure they are spending their time wisely. It is Time Management 101, but one of the biggest mistakes I see. Consequently, it can be one of the biggest tools you can offer your representatives to help bring them value.

Tip #2: Report binder for your reps

Have your team members create a binder with reports of important data they can keep in their car or at their desk. In the medical field, for example, have them make a binder with clear sheets on top accounts, top physicians, territory maps and zip codes, a list of all accounts, and business cards with dates and times of when the customer is in the office. This may seem old school as so much is electronic these days, but I do believe in having printed tools like this.

I once had a representative with major issues in territory management who was able to turn it around and become a President's Club winner. During our first ride-along together, she drove me all over the state we were in. Rather than picking a section to work for the day and decreasing the drive time, we drove throughout the whole state making weak calls and then driving back late in the evening.

Another representative did this as well… commuting 6 hours to one appointment for which he said, "I wanted you to see my territory." If you have reps with high gas receipts or mileage on the expense reports *and their numbers stink,* I can ensure you that territory management is their biggest issue.

> **If you have reps with high gas receipts or mileage on the expense reports *and their numbers stink,* I can ensure you that territory management is their biggest issue.**

When coaching reps in this area, you do not want to come across as too brash, but instead focus directly on territory management skills. Even a rep who can speak eloquently on whatever is being sold, but who doesn't possess good territory management skills, is going to have low numbers compared to other team members. Consider building a business plan for the next quarter around a specific high-volume section of the rep's territory where the opportunity exists to start doing business immediately.

The rep who initially drove me all around the state changed where she spent her time and focused on facilities in one town where she had account access. In a short span she went from being a low performer on the team to winning President's Club the following year. This kind of success story will demonstrate firsthand what a coach can accomplish through suggesting the slightest of changes in a team member's territory management, and how it can positively change someone's career.

Below are some key subjects and items that should be emphasized in this part of the report. There are multiple items that can go under this header, but these are the ones I feel are most significant:

Business planning

Business/territory planning is one of the most critical exercises you can have your representatives do. We will go in-depth in a separate chapter on how to roll out and hold your team accountable to doing an impactful and detailed plan. I recommend updating such plans quarterly and aligning them with the compensation plan and company objectives. Business planning is unlikely to be something your representatives will want to do at first, so demonstrate to them what "good" looks like. You can do this by having a pre-filled template with examples of a well-defined business plan with specifics of what this looks like.

> Remember, if you do not have this or other templates
> mentioned, they are available in the
> Skyscraper M.A.N.A.G.E.ment Academy.

In this first section of the coaching report, provide feedback on their current business planning. Whether it is using SMART goals— Specific, Measurable, Attainable, Relevant, and Time-bound— targeting appropriately, getting it done on time, or providing a stellar plan, this section is where you want to write something about this. It is important to understand why the rep is not meeting goals they set. This business plan should be a live document which can be updated if something is not working.

Expect excellence from your team members and hold them accountable to it. At the end of the day, it will make everyone more successful because of having a plan. Does an NFL coach go into a game without a plan to win? That would be

> **Expect excellence from your team members and hold them accountable to it.**

absurd, so why should we as managers be any different?

MTD/QTD/YTD Performance

Monthly, quarterly, and year-to-date performance should be documented in this section of the coaching report. It will often set the tone for the rest of the report. If the numbers are bad, the performance in the field is likely not where it should be. Make sure you have done at least a quarterly visit with your representatives and use this documentation for merit increases, year-end performance reports, and justification if you need to terminate an employee. No matter what, it will make your life so much easier if you have good notes and intangible and tangible details of performance.

For example:

> *"Jane, in Q2 I rode with you on May 16th and 17th and you were 80% to quota. During this ride along I observed these specific behaviors:_____.*
> *Q3, when I worked with you on August 12 and 13th you were 96% to quota and I noticed a significant amount of improvement in these specific areas:_____."*

If you do not have documentation like this when it comes to merit, performance reviews, or terminations, then you are honestly in trouble. Imagine if an employee was going to be put on a performance improvement plan or terminated but the manager did not have specifics on why this was occurring. Without proper written documentation, it could get the manager and the company into legal issues down the line. Documentation is a crucial aspect of being a manager, whether it is for positive or negative reasons.

Most sales representatives do not like to do administrative work, so items like weekly reports and timely expense filing will likely be something you will have to follow-up on. However, friendly reminders are easy to automate, but you do not want to end up becoming a babysitter. In this section of the report, make sure to document if the representative is not completing their work on time.

Expense reporting

Territory management includes submitting expenses. If your representatives submit their expenses late, then how can you properly manage a budget? Also, late expenses accrue. There is no need for this to happen if the representative simply submits their expenses every two weeks. Most managers will say that once a month is enough, but I highly recommend every two weeks. Receipts are like socks and seem to grow legs and run away. If your team members are only doing their expenses once a month, then they will more than likely lose receipts, then spend more time than necessary trying to find them, and ultimately way too much creating expense reports. You want your team members in the field, not wasting a whole day filing an expense report that should only take minutes to complete.

Tip #3: Use an Expense Reporting App

The past few companies I have worked for have used the expense reporting program *Concur.* Demonstrate what "good" looks like with your reps when you are with them by taking pictures of your receipts as soon as you get them. Teach them how easy and time effective it is to take pictures of the receipts and upload to the Concur app (or whatever program your company uses). The extra 10 seconds to take a picture then and there when a receipt is issued will save your representatives a large amount of time from searching for receipts later.

Customer service

Customer service and follow-up are consistent in every type of sales position no matter what industry you are in. The representatives who provide the best customer service in combination with effective sales skills are usually the ones who are most successful.

When you are in the field with your representative, watch the way they interact with their customers. Pick up on any cues the customers might give. For example, if a customer says something along the lines of "I haven't seen you in a while" or "I never heard back regarding (blank)," this needs to be part of your follow-up discussion with the rep.

Also take note if you are visiting the same accounts with your representative during ride-alongs and not noticing much progress since your last visit. This is an indication that they are not providing great customer service, likely not visiting that account, or targeting on a consistent basis as they should.

Not only does customer service include physical visits, but it also means that follow-up emails to internal and external customers get done in a timely manner. Document your observations of both good and excellent customer service in this section, as well as any areas in which your team members are not meeting expectations. Use specific examples in your notes.

So much of business is being conducted by email these days. If the representative is not writing notes for themselves on follow-up items to do after calls, and simultaneously there is an issue with customer service, then this section is where you would take note of it.

For example:

> *"During our ride-along, there were specific follow-up items that needed to occur after the sales call with Customer X which were not completed. Please input your call notes into our CRM system or log in a calendar date to complete needed items immediately and going forward. This will help you to remain on-task with follow-up items and provide the best customer service possible."*

When you offer such feedback, remind reps that it is impossible to remember everything. Implementing a follow-up system like this will make them more productive and ultimately more successful. Acknowledge to them that you know how much there is to juggle in their position. You simply want to help make their lives easier by using systems you've found to be beneficial.

There is an art to giving feedback! Tie it back to a relevant personal experience you've had in the past. When your team members know the coaching you are giving them will in fact make a difference in their business, they are far more likely to take action because of transparency and knowing this action is something that helped you personally in the past with your business.

Blueprint for Success:

The most important observables you must document in Section 1 are:

- Overall performance of the territory—MTD, QTD, and YTD
- Was the agenda for the ride-along sent 24–48 hours in advance and was it completed and thorough?
- Field productivity—Were appointments set up, drive time limited, and was it a productive use of time?
- Targeting—Is the representative targeting the top 20% of accounts, with the right frequency, and spending time in the right places?
- Customer service and follow-up—Is the rep providing stellar customer service to both internal and external customers? (Friendly reminder that internal customers are those that work inside your organization and external customers are those that work outside the organization.)
- Business planning—Is the quarterly business plan being done on time, employing SMART goals, following the compensation plan and goals of the company, and is the representative executing on the plan?
- Administrative duties—Are reports and expenses submitted on a timely basis?

You want people on your team who view their territory as if it were their own business. It may seem as if there are a lot of subtopics to cover, but if you

> You want people on your team who view their territory as if it were their own business.

hit the highlights of these bullet points with a couple of detailed quotes and observations, then your documentation and coaching value to your reps will be so much further along than most tenured managers in your industry.

SECTION 2: EXPERTISE OR COMPETENCY

In this section of the coaching report, notice the rep's understanding and grasp of technical and/or clinical components of the position. Is your team member making use of corporate resources and available training tools? Are they able to articulate the messaging for whatever you are selling?

It is very important for your representatives to be experts about your products in order to become a respected resource to their customers. Competition is fierce these days, with multiple competitors in various industries. For example, in the medical field, if we don't know what we're speaking about, not only will we lose to the competitors, but we'll also lose legitimacy with our clinicians and put our customers (and potentially patients!) at risk of harm.

No matter if your team members are selling a car, a cleaning service, or a medical product, they need to be able to not only understand their product, but also verbalize its features and benefits as well as how it can solve a pain point for the customer's business.

However, none of us start a position knowing everything about our product or position. From the CEO down to the sales representative, we all need to gain experience—through training, work in the field and office, and doing preceptorships with current high using customers—in order to become knowledgeable and of service to the customer.

This means *you* as well! One of the biggest mistakes I see managers make is waiting too long to work with their team members and learn firsthand the dynamics of the position and market in which they are playing. Do not feel like you need to know everything in order to get out there. Be transparent with team members, especially the tenured ones. You should want to learn from them in order to become a stronger asset. Don't be afraid to tell them that! By being transparent about your strengths and weaknesses, you accomplish two things. First, it allows the representative's expectations to more closely match what you can provide. Second, it demonstrates that you respect and value their experience. There is nothing worse than a manager who acts like they know it all yet has no clue what they are talking about. Be humble, transparent, and open to learning from your team members.

> One of the biggest mistakes I see managers make is waiting too long to work with their team members and learn firsthand the dynamics of the position and market in which they are working.

Tip #1: Get out in the field with your team members as soon as you start your position

Within the first 30 days, you want to start coaching visits so you can begin to learn as much about the business as possible and build rapport with your team. Set time aside in the evenings and weekends to set up your home office and do HR paperwork. Come on, you are a manager and you are in this role because you are not mediocre! What you do in the first month will pay off dramatically over time.

As part of evaluating their competency and expertise, make sure your representatives are comfortable presenting to both one-on-one customers and also to a whole room. Work together with your representatives on their presentation skills. This is where you as a coach can make a major impact on their career. Most people are deathly afraid of public speaking and it is one of the most painful experiences for them. Your job as a manager is to push your team members beyond their comfort zone so they can grow and conquer their fears. The more practice you give them when the stakes are low, the better they will perform later when the stakes are high.

Tip #2: Make your team members roleplay

Roleplay can take place one-on-one, at team meetings, conference calls, or at a sales training. Your team will not be happy about being asked to do it, but it is a critical training aspect that will prepare them to speak comfortably and skillfully about your products. It is much better to practice with your peers than to get in front of a customer and go blank.

Roleplaying will not make you popular as a manager, but it will help your team become dramatically more comfortable and successful in front of customers and when presenting to groups. As the leader of the team, volunteer to roleplay as well. Exhibit that you are not afraid to put yourself out there and make mistakes, but more importantly you care to practice. Without saying anything, this will create a safe environment for your team members to practice verbalizing the messaging and thus become more effective.

Tip #3: Have your team members record a roleplay via video and then coach them

Coach your team members on what they did well and what they could do better. Your team will likely hate this exercise too, but by reviewing the video afterward, they will become more aware of their mannerisms when presenting. This way they will not just have to take your word for it, but they can see for themselves if they need to improve upon something. Again, this is not a fun exercise, but your job is to provide a safe environment in which they can learn and grow, with an end goal of becoming the most successful in their business and career.

Product knowledge

> **If they do not have the answer, then remind them the magic words are: "I do not know the answer right now, but I will get it for you."**

Another observable to look out for during a ride-along is if the representative is able to answer product questions correctly. If they do not have the answer, then remind them the magic words are: "I do not know the answer right now, but I will get it for you." This seems so simple and you are probably rolling your eyes right now, but I have seen representatives try to make up answers just to get a sale instead of doing the right thing and asking for help.

Customers understand that both managers and representatives do not know everything, nor are they expecting you to. In medical sales, I have been asked questions numerous times for which I did not know the answer. It was perfectly acceptable as long as the follow-up was timely to get an answer. In actuality, it can be an advantage. In accounts where it is difficult to gain an appointment, now you have a reason to return that will bring value to the conversation.

Please do not ding your reps for not knowing all the answers. Instead, foster an environment and culture on your team where they feel open with you and their customers if they do not know an answer. But do make it an absolute priority for them to follow-up by asking the appropriate person in the company for a correct reply and communicating that answer with the customer.

Tip #4: Give reps a plan for when they don't know the answer

If your representatives do not know the answers and are in a critical or time-sensitive setting, try to set up a peer-to-peer call with someone in your company who can provide that answer in the depth the customer requires. The goal is to not only provide good customer service, but to also start building relationships.

These relationships can be built between reps and customers, between customers and your corporate resources, and even between customers and *other customers*. Customers want to hear from other customers. Helping them create such relationships will go a long way for your representatives. To help foster this kind of referral environment, guide your representative by showing how to set up this kind of call, webinar, email, or visit.

In this section of the coaching report, your ultimate goal is to understand whether your representative is competent and able to digest and verbalize information. If they are new, then look for their willingness and motivation to learn. If they are more tenured, there might still be room for improvement and growth. Use this section to provide recommendations for how your rep can increase their knowledge base.

For example:

> *"During our call with Dr. Jones, he mentioned he uses Product x for diabetic foot ulcers. This would be the time you could bring out our clinical paper on diabetic foot ulcers and speak in-depth about clinical outcomes for the use of our product. Please review this document and be prepared to speak with me about its highlights in our next one-on-one on September 16."*

This section of the coaching report is critical in monitoring the progress of your representatives regarding competency. Ultimately you want your team members to become an "expert" in their role, but with the expectation that no matter what their tenure, that there is always room for growth and improvement in their positions.

When you feel a representative has achieved an expert competency, now is the time to use them as a field sales trainer or in some capacity to help support both you and the organization by training others. It will be impossible for you to be the only resource for everyone about everything on your team. In this way you can expand the success of your expert team members by allowing them leadership experience. Most representatives appreciate the acknowledgment and welcome the opportunity to take on a new level of responsibility.

For many salespersons, becoming a field sales trainer is their first exposure to competencies necessary in management or in various leadership positions. Training vs. telling people what to do, holding others accountable, multi-tasking, and effectively giving feedback allows them to gain confidence and experience before ultimately being promoted into a leadership position of their own. Such roles are important steps and can help the overall health of your team and company.

Blueprint for Success:

- Spend time with your team members in the first 30 days in your position. Even if you do not know the intricacies of the position, you will learn a tremendous amount from your team members by doing this.

- Create a culture on your team where they will not be chastised for asking questions of you or using corporate resources to get answers for their customers. The last thing you want is for your representatives to feel pressure to answer questions without giving their customers the correct information.

- Encourage your team members to practice and roleplay. Whether it is one-on-one with you, a team conference call, or a sales training, it will ultimately help with their confidence and success when verbalizing their messaging with customers.

- Provide stretch opportunities for team leaders and those who want to grow in their career, such as field trainer opportunities. This will help for them to gain valuable insight into coaching and training their peers that will translate into skills they can use as their careers progress.

Section 3: Sales Skills

Effective sales skills are transferable no matter what industry you are in. More than likely, your company will have some type of selling guide such as Integrity Selling or Challenger Sales. There are many such guides, but it is important at the very least to know, expect, and be able to coach to the fundamental sales skills needed by a representative to be successful in their position—basic skills such as using probing questions, impactful messaging of features and benefits, and always to be closing for some actionable step in the sales cycle.

Sometimes, these selling guides make the sales process seem more complicated than it really is. Train your team on the basics—good old-fashioned selling. Then coach them on implementing the steps of the process during their sales calls so they can be as effective as possible by not leaving out a critical step.

#1 Probing questions

Asking probing questions will make any rep more effective and successful in sales than probably anything else in the entire sales process. Asking these kinds of questions encourages discussion, where a rep can gain valuable insight into the customer's true pain points. Then it's far easier for the rep to offer a product or service that can remedy whatever issues or problems have been noted.

In many sales visits, the customer is never asked to share about what they do or how they do it, let alone about short- and long-term goals for the future in their business. The person you are selling to usually knows these answers within, but it takes asking the right open-ended questions for them to verbalize and share them. If you and your team members do this correctly, usually the answers will be aligned with what solutions you have for the customer in whatever form or fashion your product or services come in. Just asking simple questions such as: "What challenges do you face in your business?" or "What keeps you up at night?" will help to understand what your customer's pain points truly are.

We all have pain points internally and externally in our lives that we keep buried inside. We do everything possible not to have to explore them—after all, they are "pain" points, not "happy" points. Not many people want to talk about what is truly at the heart of whatever is bothering them or holding them back. That is why therapists, healers, coaches, and other professionals are in demand. Change and thus action only come from verbalizing and acting on what is holding us back in life.

Back when I was new in the medical device industry, the biggest hurdle I faced was learning to ask probing questions and having the confidence to do so. For that position, the call points included multiple specialties. I was too afraid to ask questions because I was so hung up on possibly not knowing the answers and looking stupid in front of the customer. I literally would stand outside an office, too scared to go in, because I had no idea how to open a conversation. If I felt that way then—even after attaining President's Club status in a previous sales industry—think about how many of your representatives feel this way. By coaching them to learn to ask probing questions, you can truly help transform their business and confidence, helping them to be effective while simultaneously being looked at as a "partner" rather than a "salesperson" to their customer.

Probing questions should be open- and not closed-ended. It is possible to keep them broad without getting into specifics. The first goal is to get the customer talking, especially about what is important to them. For example, asking a physician, "Do you see patients with x conditions?" is not as powerful as asking, "What is your patient population and what conditions to they typically have?"

Let's dissect these questions. The first—"Do you see patients with x condition?"—is closed-ended and will result only in a simple yes or no answer. By asking instead, "What is your patient population and what conditions do they typically have?" the answer could provide a myriad of important information.

Closed-ended questions may get us some answers, but there's a big difference between revenue generated from selling one product for one solution versus being able to provide a spectrum of products to solve the customer's pain point. By learning all the obstacles the prospect faces, you may even be able to offer a solution for something the customer didn't even realize yet that was a problem. Seek to learn and understand. Not one of us knows what is fully going on in our customers' business or personal lives.

So, for you as the manager on a coaching visit, observe if the representative is asking open-ended questions. Open-ended probes start with *what, how, tell me about,* or *when.* Closed-ended questions almost always start with *do, did,* or *are you* and only prompt yes or no answers.

You would be surprised how many representatives and managers need coaching on this. You do not need a lengthy list of probing questions, but rather a small number of go-to questions that you have seen provoke meaningful dialogue.

In this section of the coaching report, take notes not only about closed-ended questions versus open-ended questions, but also if your team member even asked questions at all.

Many times, newer representatives will start conversations with a list of product or service features and benefits, bypassing the possibility of asking probing questions altogether. These calls are not productive because essentially the representative is "throwing up" information on the customer, without first establishing product or service relevance. You can take note of the customer's body language, likely doing everything to be nice to your representative and not be visibly annoyed or angry for having their time wasted.

Remember, if the right questions are not asked, then your reps will never get to the root of the issues or problems that your product or service can hopefully solve. By locating the pain points, your reps can finally bring value to their customers, and in the process create new revenue for your organization and for themselves.

Tip #1: Teach your reps to ask probing questions

Observe whether your representative is asking probing questions. No matter how well your representative is at explaining the features and benefits of what they are selling, they will not be successful unless they are able to effectively open the conversation. Give them feedback if you see this is an issue and ask them to come up with more open-ended questions as prompted in the example below. This will then hold you and the representative accountable for their progress in this area that may be holding them back from having impactful sales calls.

For example:

> *"Think of 5 open-ended probing questions to open dialogue with your customers. Write them down and practice them. We will go over these 5 probing questions on*

our next one-on-one on September 24, so please send a
copy to me before our call so I can review."

Tip #2: Coach your reps how and when to introduce marketing materials

Asking the right probing questions typically leads to dialogue in which marketing materials or a visual are then introduced in the sales call. Companies put a lot of research and effort into creating useful marketing materials. These allow the customer to see, feel, and perhaps even touch a product. This content may also include a list of indications for how and where the product or service can be utilized. Even if your representative has not yet developed expert competency, they could present this content and ask a question like: "Doctor, of these surgical procedures listed below, what ones do you currently perform?" When the doctor replies, it can allow the rep to know what questions to ask around those specific procedures such as: "What are your typical challenges with this procedure?" or "What are your typical outcomes?" By employing the marketing material, your rep can begin meaningful dialogue.

Marketing binders or iPads with marketing pieces should be used on most of your calls with your representatives and documented in this section of the report as well. If your team members do not typically use marketing materials in their sales calls, bring a marketing binder with you on the visit and demonstrate how to use these tools in conversation.

Once you've demonstrated the usefulness of these tools, make it mandatory for each of your reps to create and keep their marketing binders in the trunk of their car with portable files so they can easily replenish if they run out of materials. If your team is in Inside Sales, then make sure they have organized files on their computers with

PDFs of pertinent marketing materials. This disciplined approach to pre-call planning and preparation will make a significant difference in the quality of your team members' calls.

During a coaching visit, in the car beforehand, go over what probing questions the rep is going to ask using a pre-call template. Determine which marketing materials will be most pertinent for this sales call. Or, at the very least, attempt to logically guess what materials will more than likely be incorporated during the call. Also discuss what they would want the outcome of the call to be—closing for an actionable next step. Through this level of coaching, each representative will become more prepared, and therefore bring more value, surely growing their business and turning around their territories.

As mentioned earlier, if necessary, let your rep know you can always jump in and help during the sales call if they feel stuck. In this way you can model techniques of asking open-ended questions and employing marketing materials to jumpstart the discussion. The ultimate goal is to help shift your reps to a place where they are confident and effective on their own. Leading by example can be one powerful way to make an immediate difference for a team that is struggling.

Features and Benefits

Once your rep has mastered asking probing questions and utilizing marketing materials, now it's time to test their knowledge of features and benefits of whatever is being sold. Take note of whether the rep routinely talks about one without mentioning the other. Features and benefits go hand and hand rather than exclusively.

For example:

> *"Saying the product is 'Ten times more effective than the competition' is great, but it will be even more powerful to share how the customer can save money or time or stress by using this product. More impactful verbiage is 'Our product x is ten times more effective than the competition and thus decreases hospitalizations by y amount, helping with both the clinical and economic challenges your facility is facing'."*

It is important that your team members are able to articulate the most important features and benefits of your product or service. An action item for follow-up for coaching might be:

> *"Please write down all of the features and corresponding benefits for our product/services and send to me by October 10. We will review these during our one-on-one so you can verbalize and roleplay with me on how to use these during a sales call."*

This can be more difficult when selling a service rather than a tangible product. However, the same rules apply. Selling is selling and these fundamentals are crucial in both cases. Unless you push your team members to grow and become more effective, their results will never rise to meet either of your expectations.

Closing

When it comes to selling, closing is a requirement and can often be challenging and uncomfortable for representatives. I have seen representatives ask probing questions, eloquently use their marketing materials, follow up with relevant features and benefits, and then... *nothing!* No next step for any action, no request at the very least for the customer to read over literature, no set date to come for a return visit, and definitely no talk about closing for a sell.

During one remarkable coaching visit a past rep drove me two hours into the middle of nowhere to call on accounts. She had the science down and was able to get in front of customers, but there were no actions for closing. She was so proud of herself when she came out of the calls, but despite my coaching, she still was not able to close or move the sales process forward. She failed to see all the work and success in the first steps of the sales cycle were fruitless without the appropriate close. Therefore, after much time trying to coach her, she was terminated as her sales were dismal. Unless your reps learn how to close, they will never progress and land prospects to become revenue-generating customers.

If your team members are not feeling confident in closing, it is usually because they do not feel they "deserve" to close—, meaning they have not done a good job of going through the first steps in the sales process. When this occurs, I have observed that it is typically the inability to ask probing questions or just jump into features and benefits that is what's holding things up. This makes sense because why would the rep have any right to ask for some type of action or commitment from their customer if they were not able to identify a pain point or true need? If they have not done step #1 correctly then the rest of the sales call is meaningless. Remind your representatives to stick to the fundamentals and then continually coach them to improve on these steps and you will ultimately build a very high functioning team.

> **If your team members are not feeling confident in closing, it is usually because they do not feel they "deserve" to close**

Tip #3: Develop sample closes your team members can use

- "Doctor, when is your next case? Would you be willing to try my product?"

- "What are your thoughts on me getting with your scheduler and getting some time on your calendar to speak further about my product?"

- "Here is some data that is pertinent to what we discussed today. May I set up a time to follow up with you to discuss the material that I am leaving behind?"

- "Would you be interested in speaking with someone at corporate who can talk to you further in-depth? When can we set this up for you today?"

As you can see, these are not intense closes, but they are actionable steps that can be taken with the customer. This is what your team members should be striving for on each call and should not leave the appointment without doing so. If they are unable to close, then they will be unable to be successful in their position.

Tip #4: Be aware of the "relationship" representative

If you have not managed representatives yet or do not have a team currently, know that you will always have at least one person who says, "I sell because of my relationships." Building solid relationship with customers is of supreme value, but representatives who defensively suggest that they sell because of those relationships are often mediocre at best, and are the ones who will take you to visit the same customers during subsequent field visits until you get tough with them. Your representatives who follow the sales cycle, provide relevant solutions, and solve pain points for their customers will have strong relationships with *all* of their customers, not just a few.

You do not want to create clones of yourself, but rather make sure your team members are following the fundamentals of selling, executing, and growing their business. They will not be successful if they sell based on relationships alone, and it is your job to point this out to them and coach them through this.

These representatives, like others that will push back on coaching, typically have a deficit in their abilities, and it is your job as a leader to find their pain points as well and be a support and guide to get them to expand their mind and belief in themselves so they can actually grow and be a more successful representative. This is the whole point of coaching. The more you both remove ego and progress to the issues and action, the more productive and effective your work together will be.

It will not be easy at times. No one wants to hear that they can do better, especially when they have created these "great relationships," but at the end of the day, having great relationships should come from the ability to effectively probe and understand the pain points of the customer, effectively verbalize the features and benefits of a product or service, use tools and resources to drive the sales process forward, and then feel they have the right to close. There will be no doubt that the representative will have a strong relationship with that customer—one that is built on business value and not just bringing Starbucks to the office.

Another recent example I can think of is an employee who was competent on the features and benefits of their products, but was not able to close. During our first ride-along together, I honestly thought she was going to be one of the top representatives in the company. She blew me away with her organizational skills and her ability to speak to customers in a comprehensive manner, yet she couldn't ask probing questions to understand the needs of her customers. She carried a huge marketing binder but had no idea which piece to take out or when. The most problematic of all these observables was that she was not coachable. She exhibited the same behaviors quarter after quarter, despite in-depth coaching from the manager I assigned her. Not only that, but she had an attitude problem. Unfortunately, after many ride-alongs, coaching reports, conversations about hitting her numbers, and improving her attitude, we had to terminate this employee.

You will likely encounter representatives who have strengths in one or two steps in the sales cycle, but you will still have to make the hard decision at some point to spend the time to either coach them up or out. When the coaching reports confirm what an employee has not accomplished after many opportunities to improve, this documentation will help you affirm a decision to terminate. These situations are unfortunate. It is rare for someone who is exceptional in one area but can't make it work in the other areas of the sales process after coaching takes place. Usually they improve over time, so all of their skills become impactful. However, this is when coachability comes into play. If you are putting more time and effort into improving the representative's performance than they are, then there will be nothing you can do to help them if they are not willing to help themselves.

The need to terminate an employee will likely bother you, perhaps even keeping you up at night. You may put more time and energy into this person than needed, often neglecting others on the team because you are spending so much time trying to help this individual. But if you keep them in a position where their skill set is not aligned, then ultimately you are doing them a huge disservice as well as your organization.

Instead, give them the feedback in a direct, empathetic, and kind manner. Even talk about positions out there where they may be more of a fit. By propping up a failing employee, in a way you would be holding that person back. There is nothing wrong with being honest with yourself and then them when a situation is not working.

You want representatives who can become successful in all areas of the sales process—and if not, then you need to look at their coachability. Fill your team with the right kinds of people, and it will make your job far easier and more rewarding for all involved.

Blueprint for Success:

- Effective sales skills are transferrable no matter what industry. Becoming comfortable with the basic sales cycle of probing questions, features and benefits, and lastly closing will help you coach your team to excellence.

- Often sales representatives will have one or two strengths in the sales cycle and will need to be coached in the other areas of the cycle.

- If you are spending more time coaching someone on your team than others, then reflect on their coachability and if they are willing to put in the time and effort to improve.

- Sometimes you will have team members who are not a fit for the position. It is easy to neglect the rest of the team because of your dedication to turning around this individual's performance. If you are more dedicated than this team member, you will lose valuable coaching time with other team members and often not get the results that both you and that representative wanted.

Section 4: Follow-up Items

The Follow-up section of the coaching report is, in my humble opinion, the most important section. This is where observables for improvement are documented and now the action is going to be constructed. The art to having a successful recap and alignment of follow-up or action items from the coaching time together is to ask your representative first, "What are 2–3 things you want to work on?"

More often than not, this has typically been the same areas of improvement you noticed during your time together. When there is alignment of what both you and the representative think is most important for follow-up, then the representative is more likely to take action on these items… since they are the ones who first suggested them.

Neuroscience has shown that people are more willing to take action that ultimately leads to sustainable change when they are the ones who see, feel, or know that they need to fill some type of gap. This is very positive because if you just tell them what they need to do before they volunteer this information, then they will not feel internally encouraged to make any changes.

In this section, list these 2–3 action items that both the representative and you want them to work on in order for them to improve their sales skills and performance. Remember, this is a collaborative effort from you as the coach and them as the coachee to work together on these 2–3 initiatives that will help to improve their growth and performance.

For example, if the representative has issues knowing what marketing pieces to use and when, you could write:

> *"Focus on our top 3 marketing pieces (then list them), and incorporate them in your calls over the next two weeks. We will then have a call on (list the date) to review the progress you have made to implementing these in your calls."*

Or perhaps a representative drives too much in their territory and has a hard time focusing on one certain geographic area. You could suggest:

> *"Please come up with a weekly schedule and present it to me on our one-on-one call on (date). After we review, then implement a four-week routing focusing on top accounts, using our team's routing template for three months to see if this helps in achieving the results we would like to see in regards to territory management."*

The key after two days together is not just to bolt to the airport or leave without having any areas of follow-up or improvement. This is honestly a waste of time if there is not some type of continual growth for your team members. During coaching visits, have the previous reports on hand so you can look at items previously discussed. Make sure there has been follow-up to these items in addition to presenting new items to be addressed in the future.

You will find your team members will appreciate that you took the time and effort to not only ask them what they wanted to work on, but to have the follow-up calls and show that you do truly support and encourage their development. These calls should be positive as we are all works in progress. However, it is rare to find a manager who is encouraging and cares about their growth. This is where you, on your path to becoming a transformational leader, will in turn create transformational growth for your team members.

Blueprint for Success:

- Make sure to ask your team members first what they would like to work on between now and your next coaching visit.

- Always start with a couple of positives you observed, as it will lighten the mood and make your team member more open to talking about both what they thought they did well and what they want to work on going forward.

- As a manager, hold yourself accountable to these follow-up action items, and write the specific date when you will review these items and any progress made during your one-on-one calls.

- Keep your team members' previous coaching reports in a file when you have coaching visits with them. A best practice is to refer to them to make sure progress has been made since your last coaching visit together.

For a free downloadable coaching template,
please visit www.skyscraper-management.com:

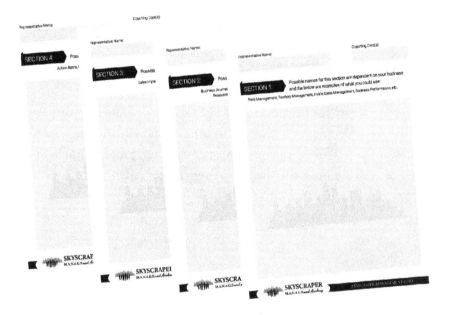

FLOOR 9

BUSINESS PLANNING

*"If you don't know where you are going,
you'll end up someplace else."*

—Yogi Berra

The other day, I got off the phone with a former representative who was on my team and had just started her own business. She was telling me about how important her quarterly business plans were to hold her accountable and have a road map to accomplish her goals. To see how an employee has grown over the years and to know that your coaching on the importance of business plans (or territory plans... whatever you want to call this document) changed the trajectory of a career will be a phenomenal moment for you as a manager, when you will know you actually made a difference. That she uses this template, in an unrelated field that is different than the one we were in together, shows how powerful business planning is.

It has always been one of my goals that team members take away 1–2 activities I have taught them, activities that made a difference and that they will use in their career long after I am no longer their manager. If you can do this, then you know you have made a difference in the larger scope of someone's professional development. In the case of business planning, I have seen firsthand how this has made such an impact, not just for one team member, but for many I have managed over the years.

So why are business/territory plans so important? They break down the goals of your team members and cultivate a road map for them, calling out key objectives they want to accomplish for the quarter and ultimately for that year. Most representatives have a large number of accounts and customers. This exercise gets them focused on the most important ones to stay aligned with the company's goals and objectives. Also, it keeps them aligned with their compensation plan, so their decisions can be made strategically, ultimately benefiting both them and the organization.

This plan also allows you to hold your team accountable to their stated goals. Therefore, under the Territory Management part of the coaching report, it is important to state the observables of whether this team member is on track to implementing a successful territory plan. A territory plan should be a "living document"— meaning that it can be changed or tweaked along the way. If a representative is not getting traction in an account, yet is doing all the little things right on a consistent basis, then you should have a conversation about changing up the plan.

As I have managed various teams in different companies, I have learned to make these plans as simple but detailed as possible. Using SMART goals, you will want to do a training on *why* territory plans are so important and then *how* to use them. Your team will likely not welcome this exercise, as they will see it as extra work. However, they will soon realize that this will become their roadmap to success, and a way to help themselves meet and exceed their goals.

> **Using SMART goals, you will want to do a training on *why* territory plans are so important and then *how* to use them.**

The bones of the territory plan start broader and then get laser focused on the execution part. Always conclude with what corporate resources or support the representative needs to be successful. This is meant to be a plan for not just the representative, but also for you as their manager, so you know how to prioritize your team's initiatives and goals for the quarter. Also, consider adding three dates for each month of the quarter, usually in the first week of each month, where you hold yourself accountable to reviewing territory plans with each representative. This will prove invaluable.

The timing of the roll out and first calls to review the plans is important as well. You want to put the due date of the territory plans on your team's calendars at least 3–4 weeks in advance. More than likely, they will wait until the last week to do the plan, however, it will get your team started thinking about what accounts, customers, and activities they want to list on their plan as well as getting them to think about which accounts and activities will get them to the performance metrics they are responsible for. In addition, it is important that all this work is acknowledged— you must follow up and go through each plan with each team member. This demonstrates it is a collaborative process and that you are interested in their plan and what you can do to help them accomplish their goals.

Also, in the spirit of collaboration, I have learned that using SharePoint or SmartSheet is a great way to keep documents in one place instead of exchanging back and forth emails. Any updates are done immediately and "live," therefore making a more streamlined and clean approach to how you are keeping key documents for your team members. Ultimately, back and forth with email and changes to documents and sending files repeatedly is not conducive to practical time management.

For example, I have a key set of reports that my team members update on a weekly basis. They simply need to open this document, make the updates, then save them for our one-on-ones. That way I can see the updates. A much more streamlined approach to document management and updates.

Sections of the business plan should include:

- Top 2–3 goals for the year
- 2–3 goals for the previous quarter
- 2–3 goals for the present quarter
- Top accounts and SMART goals of activities
- Corporate support
- Professional development
- 3 dates for follow up

Yes, this is brief, but ultimately it does not have to be lengthy to be impactful. Now, let's break down each one of these sections.

Goals for the Specific Year

It is important to understand the overall goals your representatives want to accomplish for the year. Many common goals are to meet and exceed revenue/number expectations, to win President's Club, to do x amount in Year-Over-Year revenue or growth, to grow professionally and be part of x project, or to work toward becoming a field sales trainer or senior sales representative, etc.

Encourage your team member to identify 2–3 goals for the year ahead. With more than 3, it is going to be hard for them to accomplish all of them. There is something very powerful about this section of the plan. I have seen many representatives who said in the beginning of the year that they wanted to win President's Club who later got up on stage a year later to receive their trophy at the National Sales Meeting. There is something very powerful about speaking goals and objectives out loud.

> **There is something very powerful about speaking goals and objectives out loud.**

Goals from the Previous Quarter

If you have been doing territory plans or goal setting on a consistent basis, it is important to look back to the previous quarter and see if previous goals were met. If not, then you want to discuss whether those goals or activities should be included in this quarter's plan or if they should be dropped. This type of reflection is important. You do not want your team members to plan mindlessly. If anything, if the focus is working on specific accounts, you do not want them to divert efforts. There is a trend for a representative to focus on a handful of top accounts, get business going, then divert their efforts. Only once an account becomes a stable user would it be appropriate for a representative to change focus to other accounts while still prioritizing and maintaining their top accounts. I am a big believer of slowly but surely adding medium-tiered accounts to the plan, but only once top accounts are functioning on auto-pilot. If it is a top account, it will be usually be one that will need continuous attention and support.

Goals for the Present Quarter

This is the section where your team members will write 2–3 goals for the present quarter. There will be some quarters where the goals are similar from the previous quarter. Other times there is a need to completely pivot. For example, this can include new accounts within the territory, focusing on business development in an existing account, connecting with different key decision makers in the account, or doing different activities around the same top accounts. It really is just dependent on your representative's outcomes from existing efforts—and whether they have proven fruitful. This is why it is so important for you as the manager to review these plans, as you can decipher whether goals are aligned to the success of the representative, team, and ultimately the company.

Top Accounts

The 80/20 rule seems to be consistent and relevant no matter the sales role or industry. Basically this means 20% of accounts will make up 80% of a representative's business. It should seem obvious that the 20% is where efforts should be focused, however, you would be surprised how often your team needs to be reminded to concentrate their time on these top accounts.

The number of accounts, and which ones, is dependent upon your business and organizational needs. I prefer fewer accounts, but more in-depth details and plans around penetrating that account. For example, in medical sales, a hospital can have multiple specialties. If a product can be used in multiple specialties, I would rather a representative concentrate their efforts in 3–4 accounts and call on every doctor, clinician, and C-suite member in that account rather than focusing on one specialty across numerous accounts. The accounts again should be aligned with the compensation plan, and if the compensation plan has been developed correctly, then this should reflect the overall organizational goals of the company.

Corporate Support

Having a few key notes on corporate support and how specific departments can work in collaboration with the representative's overall goals is crucial. Using corporate resources is often overlooked, but this is why it is so important to understand the overall goals for the accounts of focus, because you as the manager can help to point out how best to leverage these resources. For example, your rep could host an educational event in a target account using someone from marketing or in a leadership position to help to implement this initiative. There are multiple departments and ways that corporate can help a representative and it truly is dependent on each organization and the business needs.

Professional Development

Professional development is another part of the plan that shows you are interested in the long-term success and growth of your representative. Help your team members determine if they are interested in developing in their current role or developing toward another corporate role. Note any growth projects or assignments you can give to assist them.

It is important that team members are fulfilled in their positions, and that those who want purely development in their current role feel equally as valued. There is nothing wrong with someone who wants to do the best in the position that they are in. Not everyone wants to grow and work toward another position. It is important to understand those team members and those goals that they have for themselves. This is crucial, as if you have driven team members you want to engage them and make sure they have a runway to grow within your current organization.

Driven people will find ways to grow, and hopefully you will have the support of the company that you are with in order to facilitate this. If not, these talented individual will find another organization in which to grow. Make sure you understand the overall professional goals for your team members and how you can help facilitate their future success.

Monthly Follow-up

Include three dates on the territory plan so you will be sure to review it with your team member on a monthly basis. During the first week of the month, assess the relevant quarter's goals and determine if any changes need to be made. As a reminder, this is a living document... so there is no shame in changing it up mid-quarter if needed. The key is that you are part of this journey with your team members.

Blueprint for Success:

- Host a training before you implement territory planning for your team. This should include the "why" and the "how" on the fundamentals of what a good territory plan looks like and the step-by-step process of how to write SMART goals.

- Give your team 3–4 weeks of advance notice before their territory plans are due. Do them a favor and send an Outlook invite to their calendar for the date when you would like these plans submitted. This will give them plenty of time to think about what goals they want to include and the time to create a well thought out document.

- Schedule time during your one-on-ones, preferably within the first two weeks of the quarter to go over their territory plans. This sets a positive tone for the quarter.

- Schedule 3 dates per quarter, during the first week of each month (typically during your scheduled one-on-one call), to follow up with your representative to check in on the status of their territory plan. List this on the territory plan. I recommend using SharePoint or SmartSheet, as you can share updates on the plan and not have to email Excel or Word documents back and forth.

- Maintain a file of your team members' plans. Make sure you are observing activities that serve the goals they have identified in their territory plans. Ultimately the plans should be aligned with the company's overall strategic initiatives.

FLOOR 10

Working With vs. Against Human Resources

"None of us is as smart as all of us."

—Ken Blanchard

Working with Human Resources is a crucial part of your success as a manager. Human Resources often gets overlooked when speaking about cross-functional dealings, however you will need to work with this department in order to protect yourself, your employees, and your company during everyday management activities such as hiring, firing, performance issues, and calibrations.

There is no doubt some crazy situations will come up during your time as a manager. Your ability to work with HR on documentation and resolutions will sometimes be painful and stressful, but handling this in partnership and a professional manner will no doubt make these occurrences easier. Knowing you can trust your HR partner to help advise you in the steps should put your mind more at ease.

We covered the importance of documentation during coaching reports, but it is important for you to document consistently during your time as a manager. Your notes and details regarding conversations and situations will not only help when giving performance appraisals and merit increases, but also if you need to put an employee on a plan or exit them from the organization.

Some examples of ways you can document include taking notes after your one-on-one calls. List topics discussed and then after the call, send the representative an email re-capping the topics you spoke about and any action that needs to be taken. In this way you are not only giving feedback, showing that you are paying attention and value the conversation with the employee, but if there are issues that come up later, you have detailed notes for your records.

By sending this feedback via email, it is easy for you to keep a folder on your computer containing copies of these emails. Create a file for each employee by name and this will also make it much easier to review what you spoke about the week before. Remind your team member what they said they would do, and then talk about how they have (or have not) met these goals. Worst-case scenario, you can document that the employee is not following up on items and activities they agreed to.

> Your notes and details regarding conversations and situations will not only help when giving performance appraisals and merit increases, but also if you need to put an employee on a plan or exit them from the organization.

Unfortunately, some employees will be vindictive. It usually occurs when an employee is put on a plan and/or fired for performance yet they had no self-awareness that they were not meeting expectations in their position. The root of many issues you will face when managing people is a lack of self-awareness on their part. Or it can also be attributed to the manager not giving consistent feedback,

> The root of many issues you will face when managing people is a lack of self-awareness on their part.

not having the tough conversations up front, and letting small issues turn into large ones. You can do the best job in the world interviewing people, however that aspect of their personality is hard to identify. I will discuss this further when reviewing interviewing best practices.

If not for documentation from coaching reports and notes taken during calls and conversations, you would have difficulty justifying putting an employee on a performance plan or exiting them from an organization. These situations are the most stressful, and you may be accused of something you did not do. Never trust that an employee has your back during thick or thin. I can't stress this enough… your text messages, emails, and conversations (even in a casual environment over lunch) can and will be used against you by that kind of employee.

I believe transparency is necessary in building trust with your employees, but there are lines that can be easily crossed such as sending a funny text about someone or having a conversation about internal issues within the company. You may think it is harmless at the time, and often will feel relieved to speak with someone who knows the situation, but do not mistake this as some type of friendship. Especially in writing. Emails and texts live forever, and even though it may be illegal to record someone without their knowledge in certain states, do not think that if you are having a serious conversation around performance or an HR issue, that an employee is not recording you. Make sure to choose your words wisely and do not say anything that can get you in trouble if indeed you are being recorded.

A good rule of thumb is to keep these types of conversations brief, factual, and to the point. When you are speaking with an employee about anything performance related, you do not want to use broad context, but rather get to the point with specific dates and observables, just like you would in your coaching report.

For example, when you must break tough news to an employee, you may be nervous. It is natural to blab unnecessarily in this kind of situation. Write down bullet points listing the facts so you can read them off if having a tough conversation over the phone. If the employee wants more information—which they usually will—make sure you do not go off-script. Stick to the facts, since if you say something that may not be factual, it can hurt you later.

> When you are speaking with an employee about anything performance related, you do not want to use broad context, but rather get to the point with specific dates and observables, just like you would in your coaching report.

It does not matter what your tenure has been as a manager... tough conversations never get easier. For example, I had a conversation with a long-time employee in which the company did not approve a transfer request due to her performance. This was an individual who had gone above and beyond for the organization, and quite frankly I did not agree with the corporate decision. She was prepared to pay for the move herself. But this is one of those cases where you must be the bad guy or girl and deliver news even when you do not agree with it.

Before the call, I wrote three bullet points down with the facts and stuck to that verbiage. This kept me on-script to reiterate only those facts that were told to me. It also made it very easy to document the conversation afterward. I wrote myself an email documenting what we discussed. Writing an email right after the conversation time stamps the details and highlights accuracy.

Remember, while you are documenting things, others are usually not. This will make all the difference later when someone says that you said and did something contrary to what really happened. If you have documentation from that date and time... and the other person does not... then it makes it very hard for them to come after you.

It can often be a challenging experience depending on the staff in the department and in particular the head of HR. I have seen some truly horrible Human Resources personnel and always recommend you use your judgment as well as guidance from your manager when making important hiring or firing decisions. There is one very special HR person that would have gotten me and the company in possible lawsuits if I did not know better and questioned her on her guidance. Please refer to your manager if you feel like the guidance you are getting is not correct.

One aspect to working with Human Resources that is often forgotten is that their #1 job is to protect the company. I have had to learn this lesson the hard way. Earlier in my management career I thought HR was there to protect every individual person in the company. In theory, that is their role, but in reality it is the company that is prioritized. I have worked with HR leaders who have relayed confidential information to the CEO, creating a very difficult situation. Begin by knowing that whatever you relay to Human Resources could eventually be shared to others within the organization. I am not suggesting that you don't reach out to Human Resources for support if needed, but you should be discerning and cautious when doing so. If you have a grievance, come prepared with dates, times, and details, ready to share. Again, keeping concerns broad will not be as impactful as coming to a meeting with the facts and documentation in hand.

Working with Human Resources does not need to be a negative experience. Many strong HR personnel are empathetic, especially with newer managers and during layoffs or putting team members on performance improvement plans. When exiting people from an organization, HR's collaboration is crucial to making this process one that is respectful for the employee as well as protecting yourself and the company. They usually have very different personalities than those of us in sales, but it is crucial to make an effort to work together with these very important team members.

Tip #1: Become an active and detailed documenter

If there are only 1 or 2 action items that you take from this book, make this one of them. I learned the importance of documentation the hard way as complaints will come up. If you do not have proper documentation it can cost the company a large amount of money from legal fees, and it can ultimately cost you your position. In many instances you can also be personally libel as well. A good manager knows how to document and does it daily. Do not get lazy with this aspect of the job, because as soon as you do, more than likely something will come up where you wished you had been more diligent. The only person you can trust is you, so always remember to protect yourself rather than relying on other employees or your company.

Tip #2: Send your employees recap emails after calls

Document your one-on-one calls by sending your employees a recap of topics you addressed during the call as well as follow-up items. This will ensure that you are making progress week to week and is a way in which you can save documentation, both positive and negative about that employee. Maintain a file on your computer where you save these notes each week.

Tip #3: Do not write anything that you wouldn't want the CEO to see

Do not write anything via email or text message that you wouldn't want the HR department or the CEO of the company to see. It is easy to lose your guard when you get close with your employees. Be careful not to cross the line and write inappropriate (even if mild) texts—even if it is meant to be light and funny. Texts and emails last forever. Do not think your employees won't use this against you someday.

Remember, with sites like LinkedIn, your current and future employers can see what you post and write on social media as well. Use caution and your best judgment if you feel the need to post your thoughts publicly. Also, consider what you post on Facebook and Instagram. Many employers will monitor social media accounts of their employees. Even though this is an invasion of privacy, just keep this knowledge in the back of your mind. You do not want to post anything publicly that your employer can see, and if you do, bear in mind that your pictures and

{ bear in mind that your pictures and words are a representation not only of yourself }

words are a representation not only of yourself. The company will look at it from their point of view that you are also a representation of their organization.

Blueprint for Success:

- Documentation is key. A best practice is to take notes during your weekly one-on-one calls and send a recap email afterwards. This will both document the conversation as well as help keep your representative accountable to accomplishing what they agreed to during the call.

- If you have to have a tough conversation with an employee, write the facts of why you are having the conversation down beforehand as it is easy to get nervous and forget why you are having the conversation. After the conversation is over, immediately email yourself the details of what occurred. It is very hard to fight facts.

- Be cautious of developing close friendships with your employees. I have seen many managers cross this line and it is extremely difficult when an issue comes up with this employee later.

- With social media being so prevalent these days, be cautions with what you share in public. This can always be seen by someone in your company.

- Never forget, HR's #1 job is to protect the company. Be discerning with what you share with them. If you have any grievances, make sure to have the facts and documentation to support you. Know this information could possibly be shared with the CEO or leadership in the organization.

FLOOR 11

Interviewing

"Time spent hiring is time well spent."

—Robert Half

One of the most important parts of being a manager is making sure to hire the right employees into the organization. It is extremely satisfying when the employees you have hired thrive and become positive contributors to the company. It will bring recognition not just for that employee, but also for yourself as the hiring manager.

> One of the most important parts of being a manager is making sure to hire the right employees into the organization.

On the flip side, when you hire someone who is not a good fit, it can be seen as a negative. This is why it is so important to take your time during this process, not to hire too quickly, and to ask others in the organization (such as your boss) to participate with you in the final interview so you get additional seals of approval on your candidates.

Hiring the right people can be very challenging, especially as many candidates employ recruiters, resume writers, and other types of services that help them to nail interviews. Every candidate usually tries to put their best foot forward, so you must try to break through the façade of well-rehearsed answers to really understand what this candidate could bring to the table if given the position.

Before the interview starts, it is important to meet with whatever recruiter your company works with. They must clearly understand the job description and what type of employee you are looking for. Consider the type of candidate who is going to work well with you as the manager, who will make a positive impact on the team, and become a helpful contributor to the company's culture.

For example, I have worked for both large and small companies. There is a specific type of personality type or background of an individual who prefers one or the other setting. Someone who previously worked for a $6B company might not do well in a small company unless they wanted to make a drastic change. Especially in sales, these types of candidates have likely become accustomed to having a tremendous amount of support with multiple layers in a big company. Knowing your avatar, target the type of employee you expect will thrive within your company's culture.

Be wary of recruiters who try to rush you in the hiring process. They typically receive a percentage of whatever base salary will be earned by the candidate you are recruiting.

When I interview candidates, I like to first start with a phone or video call. These days, with the ease of Skype and Zoom, you have the possibility of a virtual face-to-face interview without the cost or encumbrance of having to travel. Do not spend your time traveling all around to meet with candidates for first interviews. This is a waste of time. Your first goal should be to narrow your search to 2–3 candidates that you will want to meet in person on the same day. The last thing you want to do with your busy schedule is to waste days traveling to meet with candidates for the first interviews, or paying to have them come to meet with you.

Most companies have standard interview guides that you want to follow in order to ask consistent questions from one candidate to the next. I always keep a copy of the guide. Some companies make it mandatory to ask every question in the guide and submit answers to HR after the interview. What I typically do is look through the interviewee's resume and write down questions pertinent to the experience of the individual to gain more insight and then move to questions from the guide. I do not ask all the questions from the guide, but rather circle the ones I feel are most important. This all depends upon the expectations of Human Resources and your manager.

> **Anyone can write down that they had territory growth, but do they have the detailed answers, explanations, and documentation to back up these claims?**

Whether it is using the STAR method (Situation, Task, Action, Result) for responses, you want to look at specifics around the candidate's answers. Often, you will receive only broad answers at first. You will need to dig deeper to get more details. If you continue to ask for more specifics, yet still do not get satisfactory answers, then this is not the candidate you want to pursue. Anyone can write down that they had territory growth, developed relationships, led a team, was a field sales trainer… but do they have the detailed answers, explanations, and documentation to back up these claims?

When I review a resume, I look for specific numbers. For example, if the candidate says they grew their numbers by 25% YOY, what was the starting number and what was the ending number? A broad "25%" may mean totally different numbers to you than it does to the candidate.

Also, notice if they have moved around every 1–2 years, have shown career growth, or if there is a track record of success and consistency in their resume. Speaking for the medical sales industry, longevity has almost become extinct. I have had to lay off employees, and have been laid off myself multiple times over the years. You should not hold that against the employee, but it is important to clarify the circumstances when reviewing their resume with them. There are certain industries where working at one place for 10-plus years will never happen again and so therefore it should not be expected.

Also, you want to review if someone has been at a position for too long. Have they shown no growth in numbers or self-im-

> look for people who are driven, who want to grow in their career and who have tangible evidence of their past successes

provement, comfortable being mediocre? It depends what you are looking for, but I always want people who are hungry and wanting to develop both personally and professionally in their lives. Bringing on a new employee who feels comfortable with not delivering needed results will set a tone that mediocrity is acceptable on your team. Instead look for people who are driven, who want to grow in their career and who have tangible evidence of their past successes and projects they have worked on.

I can't tell you how many times I have been fooled by people, so don't get down on yourself if you make a bad hiring decision. It happens to the best of us. What is most important is that you reflect upon this decision and come up with solutions for the next time. Also, it is important that you act quickly to exit this employee from the organization. It is one mistake to make a bad hiring decision, but it is a bigger mistake to keep that individual with the company longer than they should be there.

One way that I discern the accuracy of what candidates are telling me is by asking them to bring a "brag book" to the interview. I recommend this practice for both salespeople and managers. Make sure to save and print details of any positive emails or projects that you have worked on. You never know when you may need to interview for a new position. Keep a binder with clear sheets and just store these positive representations of your work together in one spot for a rainy day.

If you are interviewing candidates for sales positions, they should know about having a brag book, but tell the recruiter you would like for them to be prepared with this for the face-to-face interview. Typically, I ask to see this during the second interview when meeting in person.

After I narrow my search down to 2–3 candidates, I like to have in-person interviews where the representative puts together a business plan for their territory. Those 30-60-90-day plans are generic and usually regurgitated from one company to the next, so look for details that pertain to your specific business and company. This will show that the candidate did their due diligence for the interview.

When I ask for a 30-60-90 plan, I am looking for a few things. What relationships does the representative actually have and could they call on these customers tomorrow? Are they strategic when formulating the plan, and what actions would they take if given the position? Are they detailed oriented with numbers, dates, and using SMART goals when developing the plan? How are their computer skills? They do not need to be the world's best expert at Excel or PowerPoint, but you want to make sure they are at least competent. Did they proofread and spellcheck the plan they made for you? If not, this shows a lack of attention to detail, and overall it's lazy. Do you want someone like that on your team? Imagine if they do not spellcheck for a document such as their resume and plan, then they are unlikely to spellcheck an email to a customer.

If a candidate looks too good to be true, they probably are. Do your due diligence when interviewing and ask for specific details and documentation. Seeing the tangible output via the brag book, letters of recommendation, or anything else in writing will help to discern whether this person is legitimate or not.

As I mentioned earlier, a best practice is to invite 2–3 key people within your organization that work closely with sales to participate and accompany you during the final interview. Another option is to invite the interview candidate to ride along or sit with one of your representatives to observe what the job entails. Then ask your current employee for feedback about the candidate afterward. Pick one of your most tenured and respected team members who will be a positive representation of your company. There are two benefits from doing this. First, your candidate will get to see a day in the life of one of your team members to help determine if this position is truly a good fit. And second, your current team member will feel respected and appreciated.

I usually recommend holding 2–3 interviews with a candidate before hiring, as anyone can do well during one interview. Just like field visits, anyone can pull it together for a single day, but consistency across several interviews will make you feel more secure and confident in this candidate's qualifications and experience. Even the most tenured managers should have others involved in the process. Getting multiple perspectives will help you to make the best decision.

There should be key questions around the most important attributes you are looking for from your representative. Select your questions carefully as you want to make sure your candidate has experience working in a team environment, is coachable, accountable, has integrity, and is honest and hard working.

{ *Listen to your gut!* }

It took me a long time to do this one simple exercise, even though it cost no money and took no training... *Listen to your gut!* Listen to both your gut and the little voice in your head. Your internal voice is usually correct, though we spend most of our lives trying to shut this part of ourselves down. Your intuition will help with long-term decision making and overall success in both your personal and professional life.

If you feel off when interviewing someone, no matter how great their resume looks, really listen and investigate this internally. If I would have done this in the past, it would have eliminated much pain and suffering. No one wants to have

{ **Your intuition will help with long-term decision making and overall success in both your personal and professional life.** }

made a bad hiring choice, but the best action you can do for yourself and the person you hired is to separate as soon as you know it is not going to work, preferably during the 90-day probationary period.

Interviewing, hiring, and training someone is time consuming, no matter what level of tenure or experience they have. Take your time. Make sound decisions and be aware of any biases that you have. We all want to say that we are not biased in any way when hiring, but it is hard not to want to hire someone who reminds you of yourself. If you like yourself, which I truly hope you do, how could you not want to hire someone with your same personality traits, hobbies, or background?

Understanding your own personal biases will be instrumental in hiring others who may not be like you, but who can do the job well. Usually it is a positive, as your team will include people with different strengths and perspectives. They will also bring different ways of doing things and make your team more balanced and thus be able to navigate various scenarios in ways in which they can learn from one another.

Blueprint for Success:

- Work closely with a recruiter before you start the interview process and share the job description and any intangible aspects of the candidates that you are looking for who would be a good fit for the company.
- Bad hires happen. The key is to exit them as quickly as possible, especially if they are still in the 90-day probationary period (if your company has this).

- Make sure to use some type of interview guide, where you have consistent questions. Take notes and ask the candidate for specific details when answering.

- On the second interview, ask the candidate to bring a brag book to show tangible evidence of past successes.

- On the final interview, request a 30-60-90-day plan to see how the candidate thinks strategically. Seek to understand the relationships they have, and to learn what they would do to make an impact if given the position.

- Be aware of your personal biases. Be open to hiring different personalities than yours, rather than trying to look for a candidate who reminds you of yourself.

5

PART FIVE

M.A.N.A.G.E

G.S.D-
Getting Stuff Done

FLOOR 12

PRODUCTIVITY

"Productivity is never an accident.
It is always the result of a commitment to excellence, intelligent
planning, and focused effort."

—Paul J. Meyer

Multi-tasking and being able to juggle many thoughts, activities, and initiatives at a single time is crucial in order to be successful as a manager. On any given day you will be jumping on multiple calls about various subjects. Having to simultaneously keep up with administrative duties can be daunting while having to travel if you are a field manager or are dedicating yourself to coaching your team in the office.

A manager has to be able to do all the activities successfully in order to manage up and manage down. This phrase has always seemed a little condescending to me, but there does have to be a healthy balance. You will have to equally be good at supporting your team and your boss. Successful managers are able to both, which really is a talent. Frequently, a manager excels in one direction, up or down, and that gap is what can keep someone stuck in their career. A healthy balance will have you continually growing, thus moving up the corporate ladder if this is your goal.

After becoming a leader who manages managers, I finally saw the struggle of directors who navigated successfully, earning the support of their team, but needed to be just as efficient with higher level initiatives and projects expected of them from their immediate supervisor. They tended to get stuck in the thought process that if their team liked them, was producing, and was making their numbers, then that was all that mattered. This may be sufficient for individuals who do not want to grow in their careers, however, if you do want a skyscraper career, then I highly suggest paying attention not only to the needs of your team, but also to the needs of your boss and the organization.

> if you do want a skyscraper career, then I highly suggest paying attention not only to the needs of your team, but also to the needs of your boss and the organization

> Having the self-awareness and the acumen to understand what needs to be done both for your team and who you report to is the difference between mediocre and excellent management

This will go a long way to proving your value, as your boss may not necessarily communicate that support is needed, but it is. Just like you, they need tasks to be done on time, done well, and with a higher level of acumen and detail. This is part of G.S.D. Having the self-awareness and the acumen to understand what needs to be done both for your team and who you report to is the difference between mediocre and excellent management of oneself in a corporate setting.

G. S. D.—Getting Stuff Done—is something that is rarely mentioned, but it is important for time management. Throw traveling into the mix and then it is absolutely essential to understand how to prioritize, prepare for the unexpected on the road, and also take care of yourself on top of that.

How many times have you heard: "Ever since I started traveling I have gained 10 pounds"? It is easy to put the needs of others and the organization in front of your own, especially at the beginning of your management career. After many years, however, I realized the organizations I worked for were never thinking about my health, how many extra hours of work I did, or the events that I missed in my personal life. The company is thinking of their bottom line, so if you do not prioritize your own health and personal life, no one else will.

> The company is thinking of their bottom line, so if you do not prioritize your own health and personal life, no one else will.

For those already on the path to becoming "road warriors," this section of the book may seem like a no-brainer. However, I have learned many lessons that I wish I would have known at the beginning of my career. Bad habits can be heightened when traveling for work. The inconsistency of not being home every night comes into play. You will need a healthy mindset and dedication whether in the office or a hotel. If not, the stress can add up quickly. Being aware of your triggers—situations that cause you to make unhealthy choices—can help you to remain disciplined and therefore dedicated to being your best self.

You should want to live the most healthy and productive life you can, both on and off the road. Stress is part of every job and present no matter what we do. However, the way we process and navigate stress can mean the difference between a healthy and unhealthy life. Vices such as having alcohol every night by going to the lobby bar, overeating at dinner because you did not have time to eat during the day, or spending all your free time alone in your hotel room watching TV to decompress are behaviors that will inevitably catch up to you.

> the way we process and navigate stress can mean the difference between a healthy and unhealthy life

I have found that self-awareness of these choices helps me to make better ones. Much of this centers around how I prepare for trips. If I take the time to pack my workout clothes, wake up an hour early to do that workout, research where my hotel is located and find one near a Whole Foods or somewhere I can pick up something healthy, and pack my vitamins before the trip, these little things add up to living healthier on the road.

Learning how to plan your week on the road will be absolutely critical to having the sanest life inside a very insane environment. Basically, this section is really about controlling your controllables.

Planning the Week

Whether you are on the road or not, how you plan your week is very important. The bulk of your time should be spent observing and coaching your team members. This is why I have kept a very tight schedule and set boundaries, so my team knows the best days for calls and also when to reach me.

On Mondays, I start off the week as though I am being shot out of a cannon. Schedules for one-on-one calls are consistent—I have an hour with each of my directors where we review their goals and achievements from the previous week, their key appointments and goals for the upcoming week, any major obstacles, and what I can do to support them.

Personally, I have had to pivot and manage both representatives and directors simultaneously at various times in my career. Managing one or the other is time consuming, but managing both directly can be overwhelming. Being able to find the time to personally communicate with each individual means having to think my weeks out very carefully. Usually, this means that the majority of my Mondays are one-on-one calls. I am able to set an agenda so they are prepared with the reports I want to go over and update me on key information. This change has allowed us to be more productive—30-minute calls vs. one hour. A best practice is to send the agendas for the one-on-ones on Fridays, so your team members have time to prepare. This gets the whole team, including myself, prepared and ready to execute for the week ahead.

In addition, there are key reports that are critical for any business. Typically, these are centered around the KPIs (Key Performance Indicators). This can include reports and updates on key accounts, revenue reports, MTD performance measures, or anything that you feel is important for you as a manager to understand. The expectation is that your team needs to have all of these reports updated and ready to share.

Lately, I have been using SharePoint and SmartSheet, which are documentation systems where key reports are stored "live," so they can be updated by team members. You simply open the program to see any changes. This is a productive way to start the week. I highly recommend doing this on Monday instead of Friday because key initiatives or actions are often brought forth during this time. You can get answers that will help them start their week out on the right foot.

As far as team conference calls, I do think it is important to hold these on Monday as well, instead of Fridays. This is a chance for the team to come together and review top initiatives for the week, anything that needs to be completed, and best practices.

I have found Fridays are good days for follow-up calls with cross-functional counterparts. I try to give myself at least one office day (Monday), then Friday can be a travel day or one in which I am working on projects. It depends on your position and what the expectations are from your immediate supervisor.

For the bulk of the week, Tuesday through Thursday, I am usually on the road doing field rides or attending meetings. During my days as a district or regional manager, I usually left on early morning flights on Tuesday and took the last flight home on Thursday night. As I have gotten older, those early morning flights have gotten tougher. Now, I leave on a later flight Monday evening and come home Thursday night or even Friday morning. Remember, the goal is to have two full days with your team members and to not leave early. Not a day and a half, but two full days. As I mentioned earlier, anyone can put together a good one day in the field. But in two days, you will get a much better feel for their true time management and productivity.

Plan Your Week on the Road

It takes a certain amount of dedication to plan appropriately for working on the road. Everything from the electronics, files, and marketing pieces that you bring with you can affect your productivity. For example, I always take at least an hour to make sure I have what I need and prepare for the week ahead. In one uninterrupted hour on Sundays I can prepare my files and print out templates for my one-on-ones, plan for travel by having all of my electronics ready, and ultimately feel calm when starting out the week. If I am going to be working with a representative, I will have their file with me, along with their agenda for the coaching days, their territory plan for the quarter, and their previous ride-along reports. In this way I am making sure I see improvement when we are working together. Also, I bring a marketing binder with a notepad so I can take notes. Even as a manager, you want to be able to demonstrate what "good" looks like and make sales calls collaborative.

In regards to your health on the road, I have found it helpful to pack healthy snacks so I am not eating junk. Taking time to pack snacks, select a hotel with a gym, and make extra room in the suitcase for workout clothes will give you a great way to blow off steam. Also, you can download apps that have exercise classes. This is a terrific use of time when you get back to the hotel at the end of the day. It will become tempting just to want to go to the hotel or lobby bar, however, I highly suggest putting your briefcase in your room and, at the very least, go for a short walk. Go see something new and take that time to decompress.

In those quiet moments of the morning or evening, consider meditating to calm the brain and re-energize. I began this practice about five years ago and it made a tremendous difference in how I processed work-related anxiety. It gives me clarity and peace. If you do it in the mornings, it can also bring a focus to the day. With the influx of meditation apps, it has become even easier to engage in this activity.

Getting work done in open moments

One tip that is key when traveling is to make the most out of downtime. For me, this is when I am in the airport or on the plane. On the way to a destination, take the time to prepare on the plane, especially if you are giving a presentation.

On the way back home, skip the movie. It is easy to want to decompress, but those hours on the plane are essential to avoiding hours at home playing catch-up. Expense the $8 or $9 dollars if you can and get in-flight internet so you can catch up on emails. This is the time when I like to complete coaching reports as the information is fresh. It can take a solid 1–2 hours to put together a comprehensive and detailed report. Because a coaching report should be given, at the latest, up to 7 days after the visit, this is a great time to complete this important task.

I have found when I take advantage of that downtime I can then be fully present when I am at home. Doing the little things such as these add up to a healthy and balanced manager… one who will be in good health, mentally and physically, both on the road and at home.

Blueprint for Success:

- Take an hour before your trip to review the representative's file. Make sure to have their previous coaching reports, their territory plan, and the agenda for the field visit.
- Bring your marketing binder, updated with all materials needed, and a pad in which to take notes.
- Do your research on hotels that have gyms, and are close to a source of healthy food so you can take care of yourself while on the road.

- Take the downtime at the airport to catch up on coaching reports, preparing for presentations, and any other administrative tasks needed so you do not have to worry about doing these things when you get home.

FLOOR 13

OBSTACLES ARE OPPORTUNITIES

*"Success is to be measured not so much
by the position that one has reached in life
as by the obstacles which he has overcome."*

—Booker T. Washington

Empathy should not only be practiced with your team, but also with yourself. I can say without a doubt that when I look back upon the mistakes I have made as a sales representative and manager, those opportunities gave me the chance to learn and develop at a more rapid rate. By no means am I perfect, but I am coachable. This helps me bounce back a lot quicker from a setback.

> **Let your obstacles in life become your opportunities for growth.**

When thinking about obstacles, whether it has been personnel and personality conflicts, not hitting the numbers, screwing up a presentation, or losing my temper, it has always led to growth as a manager and as a person. Let your obstacles in life become your opportunities for growth.

Obstacles will either cause you to want to quit or they will become catalysts for learning. When you can see them merely as detours rather than roadblocks, you will better be able to move forward step by step. Think of the 3 P's—Pause, Process, and Progress—when faced with both personal and professional obstacles.

The 3 P's

Pause

When something comes your way that looks like a negative, pause before reacting. This took me a long time to learn. For example, I once had a representative who yelled at me, completely disrespectful and insubordinate. It caused me to react right back, not using the tone I should have. If I would have paused and taken a breath, I could have thought through a better response. Better yet, I would have made no response at all.

I am self-aware that I am triggered by being snapped at or yelled at. Now when put in a situation like this, I do not say anything at all. When provoked, there is more power in remaining quiet. The matter can be discussed another time when the other person is calmer. Often, this completely derails the one who was yelling. They are typically looking for a fight. At that point, the issue is more about them than you.

> **When provoked, there is more power in remaining quiet.**

Tip #1: You have the right to remain silent

When your team members become angry, frustrated, and upset, the issue is usually not with you. The issue is with them. Do not act when being provoked. There is more power in silence than there is by combating bad behavior with more bad behavior.

The source of the frustration might be obstacles related to not hitting a quota or launching a strategic initiative and not seeing results. Again, the power is not in reacting or pivoting impulsively. Resources, time, and work have been spent on launching these initiatives. If something is not working after a period, then it is time to process.

Process

Once you have paused and reflected, then it is time to process. Processing allows you to look at all the numbers, often presenting black and white results that cannot be argued. When I launch an initiative, I like to keep track of the numbers so I can see whether the results have been positive. For example, I keep a spreadsheet of the numbers before and after a webinar or presentation for an account. Was the time and effort worth it? Are the strategic initiatives producing the results that we need?

One can rarely fight with numbers, so this makes it much easier when deciding to pivot in another direction. If you are seeing the numbers, but not at the pace you would like, then think about what could be done to accelerate them. Or examine the efforts being put into the initiatives. Are your representatives aligned, do they understand the initiative and what is being asked of them, have you gotten their feedback, and in the spirit of collaboration have you asked them what they think the issues may be? Your team members are on the front lines and they are the ones closest to the customers. When processing what to do next, make sure to include their feedback in the decision making.

I also believe in having mentors, and this can include more than one person. I have had a trusted mentor for years who has a similar personality to me. This is someone I can bounce ideas off, where we think very much the same and have similar management styles. Consider finding a mentor with a different perspective as well, as this will help you learn to think differently and consider alternatives when processing. It is important to choose a mentor that you respect, someone who has been successful and is genuinely interested in your growth and development.

When processing, I recommend "white boarding" ideas or simply just brainstorming. Run these ideas by your mentors and get their feedback. This will help strengthen your weaknesses and skills that are not innate. For example, Operations was not my strong suit, however, it is key to the success of an organization. I studied Six Sigma and asked to work with Operations more closely so I could learn from them. Ultimately, it has made me a more well-rounded leader and pushed me outside of my comfort zone.

Also include your boss in the discussions. Hopefully, you have a relationship where you are not put down for ideas or out-of-the-box solutions. If anything, as a boss myself, I respect when my direct reports come to me and say something like: "For three months we have not hit our number. I am at a loss about what is going on. Can you help me process what to do here?" This type of collaboration is very important as it shows that you respect your supervisor's input, and that you are solutions-oriented and dedicated to turning around poor performance.

Tip #2: Examine the data

When processing to determine whether to continue on the same path or to pivot, look at the data. It will help make that decision easy. Numbers rarely lie and will support you in your decision making.

Tip #3: Talk with your supervisor

Speak with your mentor or boss about possible solutions to overcome the obstacles you are facing. Brainstorm ideas and work in a collaborative manner to get through whatever issues may arise.

Progress

Once you have properly processed the issue at hand, and run your strategy by your boss, then it is time to progress. When you have the data and a strategic plan using SMART goals, then act. Progress does not necessarily mean just for strategic initiatives or ways in which to grow numbers.

This can also mean dealing with personnel issues. Earlier I mentioned learning not to respond immediately to someone yelling at me. By remembering to Pause, Process, and Progress, when the same issue came up again with this individual, the second time I did not react. Instead I paused, took a breath, and said that the tone was unacceptable, and I was going to do her a favor by getting off the phone. Next, came a long, crazy text message. I did not respond. I was new to this type of behavior, but my boss had great advice. She said to go quiet. It was important not to give attention to the bad behavior. Instead I waited to Monday to finish the conversation. The employee of course apologized. During my Processing, I had documented the Friday conversation. In the Monday talk, I said that I appreciated the apology, but informed her that since this was the second time this behavior occurred, I was writing it up in her file. She understood and appreciated the conversation. From that moment forward we never had an issue again.

Tip #4: Take action

After you have properly taken the time to Pause and Process, then you have earned the right to Progress. I would rather have managers who are open to thinking outside the box and trying something new than not trying at all. If you have done the proper processing, then taking action shows a tremendous amount of strength. Doing nothing at all can be detrimental. Time goes by quickly, and if poor performance and behavior are not addressed, then it is like a wildfire that will rage out of control.

Tip #5: Action leads to progress

Whether good or bad, action leads to progress. Doing nothing does not make you a leader. Courage is a necessity as a manager and will be valued by your supervisor.

Luckily, I have never taken on an overperforming territory or team as a manager. It has always been an uphill battle that has tested my business acumen, temper, and mindset. Now as I am more tenured, I realized how much I beat myself up for bad decisions, even thinking about them for days and weeks afterwards. Self-reflection and coaching are important. But so are empathy and forgiveness. Not only toward others but toward yourself.

Remember, these are all just lessons that are going to propel your growth professionally and personally. If there were no obstacles, then the elevator in your skyscraper career would be stuck on the ground level. You want to get to that top floor. With every obstacle your overcome, you will get closer and closer to the penthouse.

Blueprint for Success:

- When faced with obstacles remember the 3 P's—pause, process, progress.

- Ask a couple of people to be your mentors, one who is like you and another whom you respect though they may have a different skill set that you admire.

- After you have paused and processed, take appropriate action. Doing nothing is worse than not acting.

- Collaborate when processing, get other ideas and perspectives from your team members, your boss, and cross-functional counterparts.

PART SIX

M.A.N.A.G.E

Empathy

FLOOR 14

Employee Separations

*"A change in direction does not mean
you're abandoning your path. Few paths are wide,
straight, or predictable."*

—Doe Zantamata

Terminating an employee from an organization is one of the hardest tasks you will have to do in your career. It is the worst part of the job, and the way you communicate this decision is going to be crucial, not only to how the employee views the company, but also how they view you as their manager.

No matter what type of working relationship you have had in the past, whether it's a termination or downsizing, it is important to remember a word that is not often used in business these days... *empathy*. Yes, that's right. Empathy will make your communication come across as compassionate and transparent, rather than cold or harsh. At the end of the day, you never know if you will be the one on the receiving end of this type of news. If that should ever happen, you would want someone who shows you the same respect as you will to your employees.

The most compassionate action you can do as a manager is to be up front and honest with people if they are not a fit for the position they currently hold. In fact, you are in a management position for a reason, and a true leader must make tough decisions.

If someone is **not** the right fit for a position, most likely:

- They will not make their numbers, no matter how hard they try.
- This individual will take up most of your time and coaching.
- Your numbers will go down as a result of their poor performance, therefore, raising a red flag to your boss about you.
- The employee will face financial hardship as they will not be making commissions, and in turn, your commissions will not be what they should for the work you are doing.
- This individual will lose self-esteem and start feeling bad about themselves. In many cases they will even start blaming you for their poor performance.
- Both you and the employee will become resentful of one another.
- If they do not take accountability, there is a strong chance you will end up in some type of HR situation, as they will need to blame someone else for their poor performance. That person will be *you.*

> There are so many ramifications of not taking action when an employee is not a good fit.

There are so many ramifications of not taking action when an employee is not a good fit. I know this because I have learned the hard way. Believe it or not, making the tough decisions quicker is in the best interest for the employee. It is an absolute drain on them, you, your resources, your team as a whole, and the organization. When you keep employees around that you know, deep down in your gut, are just not cut out for this position, it brings everyone down.

Now, for the positive news. When you realize you need to take action, and you do so, you are releasing that employee to find a position and work environment where they were meant to be all along. We all have a purpose in this life. Why should someone stay in a job where they will not thrive or excel, when there is something out there they could be fulfilled in?

Being a manager means being a leader. Do not be afraid or saddened to make that tough decision when the employee is not able to do so for themselves. Set them free to find what they were meant to do.

> **Being a manager means being a leader. Do not be afraid or saddened to make that tough decision when the employee is not able to do so for themselves. Set them free to find what they were meant to do.**

When it is finally time to separate an employee from the organization, Human Resources and their support will be crucial at ensuring smooth communication. Often times, they will have a script for you to follow. If they do not, then you will want to create one and send it to them to review and sign off on before you meet with your employee.

There are a couple of reasons why you want your communication scripted. First, you will be able to stay on track with the messaging. It is sensitive information and you want to keep it short and simple. Also, you are likely to be nervous when you are doing this, so having bullet points to refer back to will allow you to feel emotional on the inside, but still keep your communication as professional as possible. You may think it is cold to read from a script, but it will actually make an incredibly difficult situation less daunting.

If possible, meet with your employee in-person, especially if they are tenured. Your employee will appreciate that you respected them enough to meet face to face. If you can, have a member of HR with you. If not, then let HR know when you are meeting with the employee and patch them into a conference call so they are part of the conversation. Once you go over your points of the termination, then HR will step in and discuss the severance package (if any) for the employee and provide contact information for any questions.

You *do not* want to terminate or lay off an employee without having HR be part of the conversation. If the meeting must take place away from the office, then you will want to rent a quiet meeting room so you are not relaying sensitive information around other people.

Tip #1: Do separations on Fridays

If possible, do separations on a Friday because it will give the employee the weekend to process this sensitive information.

Once you communicate the separation, relay how much you appreciated their efforts, and ask if they have any questions. If the separation is due to downsizing and there are multiple layoffs, then the VP of Sales or the CEO should hold a call with the whole organization, reviewing points like the ones you will be going over individually with your team members.

You cannot know how the employee is going to react. Many times they will blame you and everyone else under the sun other than them. It is important to just listen. If you need to make comments, consider saying, "I understand this is very upsetting. I am here today because of my respect for you and to communicate this in-person."

You may have a fantastic relationship with this employee, but situations like this will test that relationship. Expect them to be upset with you rather than understanding. I have had this happen multiple times, and quite frankly, unless you were born without a heart, it will take a toll on you.

More often than not, I have been involved in separations in which the employee has been gracious and respectful. A large part of that will be the way you set the tone and approach. Try to picture yourself in their position—the difficulty of not having a job, yet still having a family to feed and all of the expenses that come with that, plus the blow to the ego. Positives will come for the employee, but they may not always be immediate.

No matter what their performance has been, thank them for their contributions and their work, and affirm that you know they will find something better aligned with their strengths if it is a termination based on performance. Close by saying you wish them the very best. We all will more than likely be hired, promoted, laid off, and separated from an organization at some point in our career. Be human, kind, and respect the employee as you want to be respected yourself.

Tip #2: Do not discuss the separation before the meeting

Your employees may ask that if you ever must lay them off, that you give them a heads up before doing so. Or perhaps upon receiving an unexpected meeting invitation they will call or text you, wondering what the meeting is about. Unfortunately, you can't say anything to them until the time of the meeting.

If contacted by an employee about the meeting request, you can reply simply, "I am very sorry, but I can't speak any further until we meet in person." This will be difficult to do, and relationships may be lost. But think about this as well: If you have to lay off multiple people and are not consistent, telling one person ahead of time but not the other, or if you tell someone and it gets out, then you are really disrespecting all parties involved and putting the company in jeopardy.

> **You are in a management position. If it were easy then everyone would be in leadership.**

You are in a management position. If it were easy then everyone would be in leadership.

I want to share an experience I had terminating an employee that represents one of the biggest lessons I have had during my career. For the sake of privacy, let's name this representative Joe. Joe was a kind, easy-going person who wouldn't hurt a fly on the wall. He showed great enthusiasm, however, over a two-year period, he consistently did not hit his numbers. As soon as he began to show progress, he would soon backtrack into bad habits and mediocrity. It took constant coaching, traveling to ride with him, and micromanaging to create a sense of urgency in order to see any change in behavior. I invested way more coaching into him than anyone else in my whole career.

You are probably thinking that it was obvious this employee was not going to work out, that it was a no-brainer to terminate him. Well, it was… if I had not let my heart get in the way.

Joe continued to have more bad months than good. It even got to the point where I had a very open and honest conversation, sharing that I did not think this position was a good fit for him. Joe did not take the advice, or any hint of it, and ended up shocked when I put him on a performance improvement plan.

I think the only person who was more shocked than him was me, and that was because of his reaction. Joe had a lack of self-awareness and it all fell back on me because I was the manager—the leader who should have made the decision to terminate him earlier in his tenure with the company.

It gets better. *Not.* Joe ended up going to HR, even after all I did to help coach him and keep him in a position. I then met with him face to face to seek to understand his grievances. He proceeded to tell me that this job had caused him to lose sleep. He was now heavily in debt and having troubles in his marriage, plus he was very unhappy in his life. All of this was my fault! Right?

Not making the hard decision to separate an employee can negatively affect the employee's life as well as yours. Having any HR-related issue is never fun and always stressful. Knowing someone else suffered because of your lack of courage to make a difficult decision will stay with you. I hope you can learn from this experience without ever having to go through it yourself.

> Not making the hard decision to separate an employee can negatively affect the employee's life as well as yours.

Another lesson I have learned the hard way is waiting too long to put someone on a performance improvement plan, and again waiting too long to terminate them until after they were on a plan. PIPs should only be for those individuals you truly feel can turn around their performance if they are put on a structured plan and receive extra coaching. If you have team members who have received feedback and coaching from you yet still making the same mistakes—not following up on what you have asked them to do, and on top of that are not performing—then you should not waste either of your time putting them on a PIP. Cut bait and move on, because you risk creating a worse situation in the long run.

For another example of what can go wrong, let's call this representative Sam. Sam was "highly recommended" to me by a colleague I worked with at a previous company. Sam showed great promise, enthusiasm, and was confident he could blow out the numbers if given the position. Charismatic and charming, Sam has probably become a professional interviewer.

Soon after Sam was in the field, I saw the red flags. He did not submit his reports on time, the follow-up was not there, he did not know where he was going when we were scheduled to work together out in the field, and he seemed erratic in his behavior. Again, I made the mistake of acting with my heart and not my head. *What is my colleague going to think if I get rid of him?* I decided it must be my fault that he was not making his number, because he had come so highly recommended.

All of this internal debate kept me from taking action.

It's never fun to not have things go well in your personal life, but when you combine that with a disappointing professional life—and the possibility of losing your job—then things can escalate quickly. Knowing this, I did everything to help Sam.

I remember speaking with my boss, and she told me to listen to my gut. I knew she was right… both she and my gut knew Sam was not going to work out. I needed to put him on a PIP, and did so. He was hit-and-miss with his activity and still not submitting reports on time.

Please remember that if a team member is not doing what is required of them on the PIP, then you can terminate them at any time. Do not think you need to wait the whole 30 or 60 days before taking action. When you prolong the inevitable, then what happened to me very well could happen to you. Make sure that you include such verbiage in the plan and that HR reviews situations in which you can terminate an employee if they are not meeting expectations of the PIP at any point.

The day came when Sam's plan was up. I scheduled a conference call to speak with him about the outcome of his PIP. I foolishly copied HR on the conference call invite, which made it clear to Sam in advance that I was terminating his employment.

Tip #3: Invite the employee and HR in separate emails

If you have to send a sensitive email, such as this one, I recommend inviting the person you are terminating, then cut and paste the information into a separate email to send to HR. Therefore, both parties have the conference call information, but you are not freaking out the representative in advance by telling them HR is going to be on the line.

Ultimately, what happened that day will always stick with me. I received an email from HR that Sam was going out on short-term disability. My heart sank when that email come through because I knew Sam did not have a medical issue. He simply didn't want to be terminated, and instead of doing the right thing and facing the consequences, he pulled one of the oldest tricks in the book. Not only did he go out on short-term disability, but he also did not provide the proper documentation for his leave.

Eventually, I was able to terminate him, but it gets worse… he vanished! I have no idea what happened to Sam, and to be honest, I was very worried about him. That human factor never leaves. Quite frankly I never want to lose that part of me. HR ended up having to FedEx a document to Sam's house with the termination letter, as we were never able to physically speak with him.

All that time, I was so worried about what my colleague was going to think. I wondered if I was just kicking Sam while he was down. I had doubts about whether I was being fair. I somehow convinced myself those warning signs were nothing.

The good thing about hearing this kind of story now is that you do not have to make the same mistakes I made. If an employee does not take your warnings and tough conversations to heart, *and change their behavior*, then they will not make it on your team. It is not only unfair to you and the organization, but also to the rest of your team members. The most time-consuming employees are the ones like Sam who will literally suck the life out of you… if you let them.

It is much better to move quickly than to slowly exit an employee. If you must, you can always agree on a resignation date. Say, "This is not working out and I will give you until (date) to find a new position." Just make sure you get a resignation letter with that date, so it's set in stone.

There are ways to do this so you can be fair to both yourself and the employee. About 15 years ago I had a manager in one of my first sales positions who said, "You will inevitably be hired, fired, promoted, and laid off one day. It happens to the best of us and it will happen to you. Make sure you treat people the way you would like to be treated yourself." This goes back to the golden rule, and no matter whether it is your professional or personal life, you want to be treated with respect. Make sure to do the same for those around you.

Remember, you are reading this book right now because you want to coach to excellence

> "You will inevitably be hired, fired, promoted, and laid off one day. It happens to the best of us and it will happen to you. Make sure you treat people the way you would like to be treated yourself."

and become an exceptional manager. It does take extra effort, but if you are investing the time and effort to read this book, then you are already on the right path.

Blueprint for Success:

- Exit employees sooner rather than later from organizations. They will only drain your time and resources if you do not make the tough decision.

- It should not be a shock to an employee if they are not meeting expectations. Make sure to have conversations often and document these discussions.

- If you have to lay off employees, do not give anyone a heads up. Out of respect to others and the organization, this information should remain confidential and not be shared with anyone.

FLOOR 15

LEADING THROUGH TIMES OF CRISIS

"In a moment of crisis,
reactions set the leaders apart from the followers."

—Peter B. Stark

Leading a team member or a group of people through crisis will be challenging. While writing this chapter, I was going through the beginning stages of managing a sales force through the COVID-19 pandemic. I felt like I was trying to make magic happen in a situation where we had to reorganize, asking more from a team that was already stretched thin, all while ultimately making sure their health was prioritized. On top of that, we had to make sales happen remotely even though most facilities were no longer able to purchase large ticket pieces of equipment.

To say this time was not easy would be an understatement. However, with every difficult situation that comes your way as leaders, it will make you stronger.

The 3 C's

Whether a global pandemic or a personal situation with a team member, remember the three C's when faced with a crisis—compassion, communication, and collaboration. These will help you lead your team through difficult times and also garner their respect for always putting your people first. When you put people first, the bottom line usually aligns itself accordingly.

> Whether a global pandemic or a personal situation with a team member, remember the three C's when faced with a crisis—compassion, communication, and collaboration.

Compassion

Compassion is grounded in empathy. Empathy can be summarized as putting yourself in one's shoes, understanding their situation, and being relatable to that person so they feel their emotions are being acknowledged. If we all just lived by the golden rule of treating others as we would want to be treated, then there would be an enormous shift in corporate America today. Ultimately, employees would be happier at work and there would be more trust within organizations. Leadership did not pick you; you picked a leadership position. It is during these tough times that your team will remember the humanity you showed them.

You can develop empathy by showing genuine concern. For example, during one-on-one and team calls, ask your members how they are doing. Pay attention to body language and/or their tone of voice. Ask if everything is okay.

> If we all just lived by the golden rule of treating others as we would want to be treated, then there would be an enormous shift in corporate America today.

During COVID, I held Zoom calls every Monday individually with my team and also as a group. These calls were exhausting, but they were critically important as a way to connect when we were not able to see one another in person. During these calls I noticed signs of depression, sadness, and despondence. When such signs are there, just think what you would want someone else to do. Would you want to be ignored because it might create an uncomfortable conversation? Or would you want someone to ask how you are doing?

Attempt to understand and relate to whatever situation is occurring. The way you show support as a leader can become the foundation of your team's culture. Whether it means sending masks during a pandemic to team members, writing an inspirational email, or simply having a call to check how someone is doing, just ask yourself how you would like to be treated if you were in this situation.

About five years ago, I had a team member who lost her significant other without warning. She was absolutely distraught. Quite frankly, I had no idea how she was going to bounce back from this event. She was inconsolable. I could have handled the situation one of two ways—be supportive and let the business side of things go, or take the attitude that work still needed to get done no matter what the cost. What I chose was to let the business side of things go while this individual tried to mend her bereaved heart. I checked in to make sure she was doing okay, I tried to relieve any unnecessary work burdens from her shoulders, and listened to her when she wanted to talk.

Slowly but surely, this individual got back up and brushed herself off. There are very few times that come to my mind when I have seen such courage. Eventually, she was able to get back to work and the sun shined again for her. She ended up winning President's

Club a couple of years later. Ultimately, it was this time when she went through crisis that created a deep bond between us. The empathy and compassion I showed to her was never forgotten. Equally, she has shown me the same compassion when I have had ups and downs.

There is nothing revolutionary about compassion, but it is surprising to hear all the stories of managers being insensitive to their team. Your team will never really be a true team until they feel and know that you care about them.

Communication in any relationship is key to its success. When I think about bad work cultures, it never fails that a lack of transparency and communication are usually the culprit. In speaking to various representatives and managers in other companies during the pandemic, more often than not, they commented that there was little or no guidance from their managers or corporate office on how to navigate COVID-19. Remember… a lack of communication is a failure of the leadership. Even if as a manager you are not given the answers or all the information you need from your boss, you can still communicate with your team members.

> **Communication in any relationship is key to its success. When I think about bad work cultures, it never fails that a lack of transparency and communication are usually the culprit.**

For example, when COVID-19 hit, I immediately assigned each team member a Zoom account. I am not saying that was genius, as everyone is now using Zoom as their primary form of communication apart from email. However, we were able to pivot quickly and start communicating best practices of what we could do during this time, training and learning to use Zoom for customer presentations, and sharing new ways of reaching out to customers.

I think back on companies I have worked for in the past, and when a crisis occurred, it was usually "all about the company." But stop to think about the customers you serve and what they may be going through. How do the products, services, or information that you provide match what they need right now? Customers will remember what your company and your team did during crisis times.

Similarly, if you or your team are insensitive, they will forever remember when your organization did not take into consideration what they were going through. I am not saying you should give things away for free, or that the customer can get whatever they want. Simply, be honest and state what you can and cannot do. It is that simple.

Tip #1: If your reps are anxious about making a crisis call, take time to speak with customers directly

Take the time as a manager to speak with customers or individuals if your team members are anxious about doing so. Bad news is usually received much better when delivered by someone other than the representative. It shows the representative did their due diligence and took the customer's concern to someone higher in the organization. It demonstrates they listened to their customer and had every intention of trying to help. It also makes it easier for the representative to continue a relationship with that customer in the future, even if they can't meet the customer's current request.

As a leader, it is not your job to be doing all the communication, but it does starts from you. Tone is so important, whether in email or on conference calls. If the manager sounds despondent, how is the team going to react? Email can be misconstrued, so especially during times of crisis, read them over a few times before hitting send.

We are human and just because you have the title "manager" or "director" does not mean you are exempt from feelings of grief, anxiety, or despair. However, there is a way in which you can be transparent and also not take down the team or make the situation worse. People will pick up on the language used and the energy exuded. As a leader, initiate the necessary dialogue for everyone to feel as confident as possible during difficult times.

> **As a leader, initiate the necessary dialogue for everyone to feel as confident as possible during difficult times.**

Layoffs can be detrimental to the culture of your team and the organization if not done right. When I say "done right," I mean operating according to the golden rule. Even when laying off people, do it in a way in which you put yourself in the other person's shoes. It is okay to show that you are vulnerable, that this is a difficult situation, and that this is not an easy process for either party. Don't break down or cry, but also don't be cold as steel and inhuman. The tone of your voice can make all the difference. Your compassion and empathy, your professionalism, and the way you break this life altering news will make a big difference in how the other person receives it.

Reorganizations can be another difficult aspect of being a manager. It never gets easier. The only thing that does get better is if you can learn to bring compassion and empathy to that process as well. Humanity and vulnerability are key in these situations.

Communication

Communication is also key in these situations as your other team members will end up finding out what has occurred. I have heard many stories of people just waiting by the phone, scared to death that they were going to be the next one to be called. You will start receiving text messages and inquiries. People usually have a sense of when layoffs or terminations are coming.

No matter how cruel it seems, you *cannot* tell anyone. Even if they are in a leadership position. Such staff members should realize that you can't make exceptions. If you tell one person, then it would be unfair not to tell everyone. Instead, keep the news to yourself. Simply make sure your organization has a communication ready to send out, explaining what has happened once the appropriate parties have been contacted.

One of the many times I had to do this, I first had a call with my director team. That call was really a rally cry for us to band together as leaders, to make sure we did everything possible to honor those who were being displaced, and communicating what occurred in a professional and positive manner.

In today's world, layoffs and reorganizations are happening often. Team members are being asked to do more with fewer resources. Communicate with your team in a professional, yet empathetic manner. Seek to understand and answer questions that they may have. Pivot quickly if you have to displace people and create coverage. Show your team your vision and plan, communicating via a live call. They will feel more settled in an unsettling time when they see that their leader has a plan in place to navigate this difficult situation. This is not the time to put your head under the covers. This is when leaders show up in management.

Do as much work as possible prior to any displacements to figure out a coverage plan, additional compensation if possible, and what this will look like for the remaining team. Usually, there is not much time to perform this preparatory work, but you owe it to your team to get as many ducks in a row before you have to make this type of announcement.

When this situation occurs, do not take it personally... either from comments of the person who is being displaced or the team members when you let them know. It will be more common than not for the person you are displacing to be angry and make some unsavory comments. This is why it is so important to have Human Resources involved while you are doing this. They will help the conversation flow when it really is a shocking and surprising moment for the employee.

When you have your team call, people will likely cry, be angry, and immediately start to become afraid for themselves. If it is the last layoff, make sure to assure remaining team members that this was the last of the changes that were to be made. Let them process the emotion before showing them the plan you have for coverage. Typically, wait 48–72 hours, as this will give them time to process their emotions. The emotions will still be there, but not as intense. They will then be able to accept and process the vision you have for your plan more readily if you wait this period of time.

Tip #2: Wait 48–72 hours to share a coverage plan

First, make sure the company has a communication ready by email or a conference call ready the day of the layoffs. You will want to have a call with your team to acknowledge what occurred, and that you will be following up with them in a couple of days to go over any coverage plans or re-structuring of territories. This will give your team the time they need to process any layoffs and losses that they have experienced as a team. They will be more receptive to additional changes after a couple days.

The tone, empathy, and words we choose as leaders can make a significant difference in how people manage this situation. Do not ever feel or believe that others are feeling exactly the same as you. We can never know precisely what others are going through. All we can do is relate to our own situations and how we would like to be treated.

There are no shortcuts to healing. Give others the space they need to do so. Never treat people like they are a number. Stand your ground and always put people first.

Collaboration

Many of us these days are doing more with fewer resources. It is critical that your team is recognized for the work of overcoming a crisis. Build a collaborative environment where each and every one of them sees and understands your vision as a leader and what their function is in contributing to this vision. If a leader does not set a clear vision for what the team needs to accomplish, when they eventually turn around to notice, there will be no one following. The leader will be alone, walking toward a vision that only he or she understands.

Tip #3: Share your vision and talk about it

Communicate your vision and plan, making sure your team understands this plan, then ask them what they think about this. What would they like to add? When you collaborate with others then the ideas are no longer just yours. The plan becomes "ours."

This is not just for your immediate team, but when working with others cross-functionally inside your organization. It is important that they not only know your plan, but feel part of it. A best practice is to share your vision or initiatives with others and get their feedback. A sales leader can't work in a silo. There is so much opportunity to be a catalyst to bring others on this ride with you and, in turn, to make your plans even better through collaboration.

Summary

Compassion, communication, and collaboration are essential to becoming a successful manager and a transformational leader. These intangible leadership traits will bring your team to new levels. The human aspect should never be forgotten, as we are all emotional creatures who will respond positively or negatively to the way we are treated. People will never forget when empathy is at the forefront, when they are treated with respect and not just a number. Support others like you would want to be supported. In turn, you will build a culture where your team will thrive.

Blueprint for Success:

- Remember the three C's when managing through crisis—compassion, communication, and collaboration
- Handle layoffs in a way that is respectful, not just to the employee(s) involved, but also to your team. Give them

time to process the information and then share with them your vision and next steps.

- Communicate often and collaborate with your team. Bring them on the journey with you, ask for their feedback, and collaborate with others inside your team, and also with those in cross-functional positions such as marketing and operations.

FLOOR 16

Manage the Person First and the Numbers Will Follow

"There is a story behind every person.
There is a reason why they are the way they are.
Think about that, and respect them for who they are."

—Barchandangel

I have heard over and over in my career to manage my team "to the numbers." Yes, your team members need to understand the numbers—both their individual ones and then your team numbers—and they also need to understand that their work influences the organization's numbers. All of this is very important, yet the way you treat your team should be consistent, whether the numbers are up or down, whether an employee is ranked first or last. They should be treated with respect.

Your team members will typically know when their numbers are not good, and they will also not feel great about

> **the way you treat your team should be consistent, whether the numbers are up or down, whether an employee is ranked first or last. They should be treated with respect.**

themselves at that time. When the numbers aren't there, are you going to beat them up... or lift them up?

Think about what kind of managers you have had in the past. How did they react in times of stress? How did they act when the numbers were thriving? It may sound contradictory but being a rock for your team will ultimately be the best course of action you can take. If you are unstable, scared, or feeling personally affected in some way, your team will feel it. If you instead face the numbers head on, give a clear vision to your team on how you are all going to work together to turn things around, then they will not only respect you, but they will also feel a personal interest in changing the performance. They will come together as a team and support you and the vision you are instilling in them on how to do this.

> **when collaboration takes place in a safe environment, great ideas come to the forefront**

Also, I highly recommend asking them for recommendations and to collaborate as a team on how they are going to turn around poor performance. As mentioned in the previous chapter, when collaboration takes place in a safe environment, great ideas come to the forefront. Not only that, when the team hears ideas from their peers and action is taken on those ideas, it shows they are being heard and valued.

Manage your people as human beings and give them a vision on how to hit their numbers. I can assure you they will remember anytime when you beat them up on bad numbers. They will remember it so well that it will take away from future times when the numbers are good, and you will find yourself alone.

There have been many President's Club award ceremonies when I saw a manager win an award but their team members commented that they just got lucky, or that the manager was a jerk. Take your team members on the journey with you. When the times are tough, be that solid person, the foundation on which you all can step together in unison toward new heights. Manage the individual, and remember they are a person first and not

> **Manage the individual, and remember they are a person first and not a number.**

a number. When you manage people with respect, ensure they understand your vision and the roadmap on how to achieve their goals, the numbers almost always follow.

Am I perfect? Absolutely not. Am I cognizant of this and make an effort even if I am upset about poor performance? Yes! In times of stress, your reactions can set the tone for how your team responds. You want to be a representation of a strong leader, and no matter how badly you are getting the heat from your boss, make sure your team members do not get burned.

> **no matter how badly you are getting the heat from your boss, make sure your team members do not get burned**

You do not want either yourself or your team to get stifled by it. Overreaction can become an Achilles heel. While I hope you never get treated the way some of my supervisors have treated me, if it does happen, know your rights, or consult someone who does. Then remember that it does not give you permission to treat your team as horribly as you may have been treated. Strive to be the leader you have always wanted.

We are continually building our skyscraper careers. I know the work will never be fully done and the blueprint will always be changing. Our best life is one of continual yearning, learning, and growing. Long after we are gone, I hope our work will still be there, functioning as a foundation for others to build upon.

Blueprint for Success:

- Remember your team members are more than just a number. Treat them with respect, coach them to excellence and you will see the numbers follow.

- Be a buffer for your team, so they do not feel the heat from corporate if numbers are down. This will free them to perform and not be stifled by the pressure.

- Collaborate with your team, asking them about strategies or tactics in which they think numbers can be turned around.

- Think about the supervisors you worked for, reflecting on the positives and negatives of them. Who do you want to be remembered as a leader?

The Penthouse Suite: Conclusion

It was important for me to write this book because, quite simply, I do not want you to have to go through some of the same struggles I have faced. I do not want you to have to learn the hard way how to navigate difficult situations and feel overwhelmed by stress while doing so.

With over half of first-time sales managers not receiving any management training at all, it can be daunting to take on your first team. If the experience is anything like my start in management, it would make most people want to quit, just like I felt at one point. Luckily, I had a couple mentors to reach out to, to ask questions, and to talk about what I was going through. That helped tremendously through all the difficult situations.

Hopefully, you will learn to face the good times and bad times head on. After reading this book you will feel more confident navigating the day-to-day management experiences, and be on the lookout for red flags that can alert you in advance to situations that need special treatment. As your confidence increases, you will be able to make tough decisions in a more thoughtful and balanced way.

The stress of work should not be carried over to your home life. It is not worth that sacrifice. Ultimately I hope you will also learn to take care of yourself, and to value that self-care just as importantly as how you take care of others along the way.

As the years go on, it will be difficult to remember all the places and people you have worked with. However, you will never forget the representatives who overcame personal and professional roadblocks, the people who showed courage and aptitude. Much of what you will learn about the human spirit will come through the lens of experience. There is no title or amount of money that could ever represent the honor that it will be to be part of these individuals' lives. That you have the opportunity to go on this journey with so many amazing people will be a blessing of your life.

We all make mistakes, but remember to learn from each one. Coach others on their journey toward their goals and aspirations, and help them understand that mistakes are simply stepping stones to success.

> Who you are today is not because of the mistakes you have made; it is because of the way you responded.

Who you are today is not because of the mistakes you have made; it is because of the way you responded.

I hope you will benefit in some capacity from these managerial lessons. When you incorporate coaching and coaching tools, you will be able to build the platform for your skyscraper career. It may take years to complete, but once your foundation is set, then the growth is tremendous. The sky will be the limit to what you do in your career once you master these fundamental lessons.

I started with no management experience whatsoever, probably like you, but I always kept my head and heart in the right place. There is nothing more important in your career as a manager than the people who are on your team. Remember to treat them the way you want to be treated. Nurture and help them grow. Coach and give them the time and feedback they deserve. What you will realize is that the growth will not be only with your team, but also within yourself.

Never forget your purpose and passion, and the reason why you decided to take on a leadership role in the first place. It is my hope that you will create and enjoy many great memories and positive experiences.

The foundation of the skyscraper career lies within your heart and head. The height is what you build with experiences of people and places that help you become the leader you one day dream to be.

When the dust settles,
when I am long gone,
may my structure still be there,
glistening and ever strong.

—Meghan Clarke

ACKNOWLEDGMENTS

First and foremost, I want to thank my husband Rudy for all his unwavering support and encouragement. The dreams that I have wanted to accomplish would have remained just dreams if it was not for all the sacrifices that he made to help me on my journey. Over the past two years in particular, most weekends have been me working on this book and other projects, while simultaneously traveling most weeks for my day job. He never complained and only cheered me on with these projects. Rudy, this work would be meaningless without you by my side.

To my parents, for always encouraging me from an early age that I could do anything that I put my mind to. To my mom, for showing me that at no matter what age that I could make whatever I wanted to out of life. That the unexplored doors through various phases of life are there, through faith, curiosity and "doing the work" that the impossible can be made possible. Thank you also for all the proofreads, optimism, and heartfelt feedback. You mean the world to me and I am so grateful to continue to have you as an example of both a beautiful role model, inside and out.

My family, John, Tiffany, Brennan, Shannon, Brian, Taylor, Hannah, Madison, Brooke, Vivian, Bruce, Paige, Mike and the newest member Cassidy. You all inspire me through your kindness, warmth, and graciousness to be the best version of myself.

Regina Lally, for all of your support and encouragement over the past 13 years.

My grandmother, Doris, who is no longer physically here. Your strength and determination I carry with me each day. The love you gave me and the example you set will never be lost.

For the healers, mentors, and teachers in my life that have been an inspiration and part of a transformational journey that I have made in the past five years: Peggy Gaines, Christian de la Huerta, Clare Merlo, Bobbi Gemma, and Christina Casado. Christina, through many countless talks, this book manifested itself. You have been in my corner through thick and thin, and I am tremendously grateful to you in many ways.

Will and Phoebe Ezell for helping to keep me grounded and inspired to fulfill the dreams that I have. Phoebe, for our weekly calls and work on the Skyscraper Academy. You have shown me through example the power of giving. I will never forget what you have done for me and will pay it forward. Bruce Turkel, for giving me the transparent feedback I needed to move forward in the right direction with these projects. For continuing to still be a resource and mentor. Dr. Percy Nelson, for your continual counsel and advice over the past 14 years.

To my editor, Demi Stevens, thank you for your patience and dedication with me on this book.

David Gildea, for your mentorship both as a first-time manager and today. You have always been there to advise, help, and support. True leadership and dedication have always been exhibited through your actions.

Lastly, to the leaders, team members, and colleagues who have made an enormous impact on my life and career: Mark Neidert, Gary Diaz, Jennifer Assante, Lita Lilly, Grady Grant, Kristine Steely, Miguel Echenique, Keith Keller, Dave Dorn, Vic Garofalo,

Bill Schneider, Bill Cadwallader, Stas' Skocyzlas, Bill Irizarry, Callie Neel, Kristine Osborne, Susan Breitbart, Jerome Malone, Yvette Grove, Laura Bonich, Tommie Deaner, Rachel Bouman, Mary Lou Andre, Gerry Savage, Luisa Hoyos, Alan Campbell, Otto Stoeterau and to the countless others who have made such an influence throughout the years. Without you all, there would be no meaning in what I do nor an example of what true leadership looks like.

Thank you all for helping me to build my Skyscraper.

Meghan Clarke's company, Skyscraper Consulting Group,
provides managers with the resources they need
to coach their teams to excellence.
Visit: www.skyscraper-management.com
to download the templates referenced in the book.

The Skyscraper Consulting Group has also created
the Skyscraper M.A.N.A.G.E.ment Academy
that provides step by step instructed modules,
templates, PDFs, and tools in one program
that is designed to give sales managers the tools
they need to build a successful foundation in management.
Also, other services such as Executive Coaching, Consulting, and
Speaking engagements are offered as well.

For more information please visit:
www.skyscraper-management.com

CPSIA information can be obtained
at www.ICGtesting.com
Printed in the USA
LVHW092146120421
684322LV00014B/145/J